ROSES OF PAESTUM

BY

EDWARD M^c^CURDY

British Library Cataloguing-in-Publication Data
A catalogue record for this book is available from
the British Library

EDWARD McCURDY

Edmund McCurdy was a literary scholar, linguist, and historian.

He was educated at Oxford University, where he displayed considerable literary talent – writing many essays and poems, serious and light. It was during this time, that McCurdy also developed a life-long interest in Leonardo Da Vinci. He married Sylvia Stebbing in 1906 (at the age of thirty-six), and the couple embarked on a six-month honeymoon tour of Italy.

After this, Stebbing and McCurdy made their home in the village of Ashtead, Surrey, England. They had a happy marriage, and had six children together. Stebbing was very involved in social and charity work, and one of her main interests was helping to run an Old People's Club, each year holding a summer party at their home.

One of McCurdy's main achievements was his translation of Leonardo da Vinci's diaries (with the work appearing in 1904). This was a substantial achievement, as the diaries were written in mediaeval Italian; a complex language to master. Secondly, the diaries were written in Da Vinci's famed 'mirror writing', where he penned all his text backwards (so one can only read it by reflecting the book in a mirror). In recognition of this work, McCurdy was made a member of the exclusive 'Athenaeum Club' (a private gentlemen's members club in London, founded in 1824).

McCurdy followed this text with his translations of the *Notebooks of Leonardo* (published in 1906), and then *The Thoughts of Leonardo* (published in 1907). His major work was the issue of a two-volume edition of the *Notebooks* in 1938. This was re-issued in 1948 and ran into several editions.

'Nay, ye may not liken dog-roses to the rose, or wind-flowers to the roses of the garden.'

—Theoc. Id. V.

(Lang's *Trans.*)

To the Reader
by way of
Preface

THESE Essays treat of Italy and the mediaeval spirit,—and Italy is a wayward sovereign, and her beauty leads a man far afield.

Let me say—now that the work is done in such measure as I am able — that my purpose was to trace the mediaeval spirit in deed and dream by considering some of its imaginative activities,—its questings of the ideal in art, in faith, in love, and in fantasies of things more visionary than these.

They were the roses of mediaeval beauty that I set out to gather, and therefore the leaves are named of the Paestan roses because these also were of seed of Greece and bloomed in Italy.

Now that the leaves are all placed together I know that they are but wind-flowers. Some day I hope to gather of the roses of the garden.

ROSES OF PAESTUM

Contents

Roses of Paestum

'EGYPT in her pride had sent thee, Caesar, winter roses as a rare gift. But as the sailor from Memphis came near to thy city he thought scorn of the gardens of the Pharaohs, so beautiful was Spring and odorous Flora's grace, and the glory of our Paestan country, so sweetly did the pathway blush with trailing garlands wherever his glance or step might fall in his wandering.'

And Martial asks that Egypt should rather henceforth send grain and take roses, seeing that in these she must yield the palm to the Roman winter.

The Roman winter has still its eulogists,—it is hard to overstate its perennial beauty; but the supply of Paestan roses can no longer be accounted in its praise.

The glory of the Paestan country is still a thing to wonder at. The city is set between the mountains and the sea. Behind it the wild glens wind steeply to the huge amphitheatre of the Apennines, whose jagged peaks strain upwards to the deep-blue dome of the Calabrian sky. To the north the Gulf of Salerno is broken in tiny bays, in which nestle Positano and Amalfi, and above the latter Ravello is seen gleaming proudly on its height. A meadow lies between the city and the sea, and across the bay the eye rests on the islands of the Sirens, and Capri.

The city was founded by Greek colonists from Sybaris in about 600 B.C. It remained practically a Greek city after becoming subject to the native Lucanians, and we are told that the inhabitants were wont to assemble every year to lament their captivity and recall the memory of their greatness. Posidonia became Paestum, and flourished under Roman rule. Her legions took part in the Punic wars, but her famed arts were ever those of peace. Virgil as well as Martial tells of her flowery gardens, and of the roses that bloomed both in spring and autumn 'biferique Rosaria Paesti'; and whenever Roman poets singing of the rose were minded that she should be known of local habitation, it was for the most part in Paestan gardens that they gathered her; so that the roses of Paestum became known as emblems of her beauty. Life receded from the city in the latter days of the Empire, and finally the Saracens sacked and devastated it, and the Normans, a century later, under Robert Guiscard carried off all that they could carry of its sculpture to Salerno and Amalfi, there founding cathedrals with marble from its temples. The mouth of the river Silarus meanwhile had silted up, and the plain had become a marsh, stagnant and miasmal.

The city now is a solitude. A few fragments of the ancient walls and the lower part of one of the gates remain;—yet the little that is left of what the Romans built seems new, and, like the few modern houses of Pesto, seems to shrink away in timidity before the three Greek temples whose huge colonnades tower majestically to the horizon. They lie facing the sea and the sunset robed in the awful beauty of desolation and decay,—timeless monuments of an immemorial past. Of the three, the temple of Poseidon is at once the oldest, the largest, and the most complete.

'New Gods are crowned in the city'—or were in the years before the city became a solitude peopled only by marbles and memories. New temples of strange worship were set beside this temple of Poseidon; and from these, too, the flame of human veneration has passed, and the altars have been bared of sacrifice and votive offering, and they have passed away with the passing of the life that dwelt beneath their shadow. Immutable, the temple of the sea-god has been witness of their coming and departing, and by its contrast with their transience it would seem that beneath the surges that murmur to the meadow, the god still lies in power, potent as of old to guard his sanctuary.

There is a fascination and a sense of content in the scene which is in itself a recognition of the supreme, the inevitable beauty with which nature has encompassed the desolate temples.

The sunlight is as a wand of enchantment wonder-working; the air quivers golden to the alchemy of its touch; the smitten facets of the marble gleam and glister with hues iridescent. Wild flowers spring luxuriant from the crevices of the columns; lizards slumber on the stones; all around incessantly the dry *chirp chirp* of the cicalas; and in the meadow to seaward herds of oxen wrench the long coarse grasses. Sun-steeped nature covers the footprints of the past, yet her beauty hides not—rather enforces—that they are footprints and they are desolate. Cicalas sing where once was the music of many voices; acanthus now where once grew roses; and of the rose-gardens whereof the Roman poets sang no vestige remains.

They are in thought fair to dwell upon, and they call a fair picture before us, the long festoons of roses trailing around balconies or gardens. Nestling amid their fragrance, lovers would sit at nightfall and listen to some singer from Syracuse. Perhaps as the singing ceased they would wander together in the moonlight down the long colonnades and look over the sea to the isles of the Sirens dark and tremulous in the evening air; and stay awhile, silently, hearing the murmur of the stillest wave, the one pitying all those mariners who had been lured to death, the other thinking of that strange mastering music which had drawn all men unto it until Ulysses' ship passed by unheedingly and the singers perished and the rocks were silent, wondering, may be, if the sea had memory and in its voice lived their song imperishable; and then they would turn and wander back among the roses and think no more upon death.

Fantasies—woven of dream! Imaginings—of days that are dead to memory! Yet the Greek city by the bay of Salerno must have witnessed many such scenes in the days of the roses' flowering.

As the ivy round the oak so legend twines its tendrils around history, clinging to and supported by its strength, yet chapleting it with leaves undying after that its sap has departed, disdaining or denying the touch of death. So when legend drawn by the grandeur of their deeds has twined her tendrils around the names of kings and warriors, her contest with death is not for their memory alone, she tells rather that they are not dead but fallen asleep, and that in the fulness of time they will awaken. So Arthur 'Rex quondam Rexque futurus' abides in Avilion to be healed of his wound, and 'men say that he shall come again and he shall win the holy cross'; so Charlemagne, and Barbarossa, sleeping in his mountain fastness—they will awaken, legends say, in the hour of need.

As with kings above their compeers in prowess exalted, so with the flower of flowers,

'Ut Rosa flos florum
Sic Arthurus rex regum,'

and the roses of Paestum, the roses of Greek beauty growing on Italian soil, in Virgil 'the rose twice-flowering,' 'biferique Rosaria Paesti,' passed not into memory when their gardens were forsaken. They were upgathered of the immortal spirit of beauty, and lay in slumber until the fulness of the time of reflowering, when in the valley of the Arno all the arts resurgent were one harmony of joy and thanksgiving.

To consider the second flowering of the roses we must leave the Greek city, deserted and finally despoiled by the Normans, and pass to Pisa.

Pisa in the twelfth century was the mistress of the Tyrrhene sea. Her supremacy extended along the coast from Spezia to the port of Rome. Her grandeur in its zenith is perhaps only comparable in its conditions to that of Venice two centuries later. She took part in the Crusades and had great trade with the East. She had won from the Saracens Sardinia and the Balearic Isles, and had defeated their fleets off Tunis and Palermo.

Ever Ghibelline, ready to fight the Emperor's feuds as well as her own, she warred with all her neighbours and especially with the other maritime republics. 'The mad little sea-falcon never caught sight of another water-bird on the wing but she must hawk at it'; and after the fall of the Hohenstaufen she was at last subdued on the sea by her inveterate and often defeated foe Genoa, at the battle of Meloria.

Her fleets returning in the days of her

triumph, brought back spoil and art treasure: the Pandects of Justinian from Amalfi, earth from Palestine that her dead might rest in her Campo Santo, marble sculpture from the East, from Sicily, and from various parts of the peninsula to adorn her cathedral, which she had built in memory of her victory over the Saracens off Palermo.

Among this sculpture was a sarcophagus with two scenes in bas-relief from the story of Phaedra and Hippolytus, which for many centuries stood beside one of the doors of the Cathedral. It there served as the tomb of Beatrice of Lorraine, the mother of the Countess Matilda of Tuscany who has been by some identified with the Matelda whom Dante saw beyond the stream of Lethe walking in a meadow singing and gathering flowers, and who became his guide through the Terrestrial Paradise.

The custom of using these sarcophagi as Christian tombs was not infrequent, and there are similar sculptured sarcophagi in the Cathedrals of Amalfi and Salerno.

These, together with the numerous marble columns of atrium and campanile, were undoubtedly taken from Paestum; and it is perhaps permissible—theorizing where record can neither substantiate nor confute —to assign to the relief of Phaedra and Hippolytus the same place of origin. The Pandects were in all probability not the only trophy which the Pisans carried away after their victory over Amalfi, and we know that sculptured reliefs from Paestum were there ready to their hand.

The sarcophagus, whether from Paestum or elsewhere, is carved in the classical Greek manner, and Vasari tells us that as it stood by the door of the Cathedral it drew the attention of Niccola Pisano, who was working there under some Byzantine masters. 'Niccola was attracted by the excellence of this work, in which he greatly delighted, and which he studied diligently, with the many other valuable sculptures of the relics around him, imitating the admirable manner of these works with so much success, that no long time had elapsed before he was esteemed the best sculptor of his time.'

There is nothing sensational about this statement, and its moderation may incline us to accept it without cavil on the much vexed question of Vasari's inaccuracies.

Niccola Pisano was destined to be the founder of a new school of sculpture, but he was then an apprentice, and like Cimabue in his youth, was studying his art under Byzantine masters, who were then the best exponents of the arts of design; and this is invariably the way in which genius prepares itself for active service,—there is no rupture in tradition, the old is assimilated and then the step forward is made.

He saw in the Greek reliefs a precision of touch, a feeling of dignity and beauty which surpassed anything that his Byzantine masters had attained to in their works.

Still working we presume with the Byzantines, he added a new teacher, and served a new apprenticeship to the work of this unknown Greek. Athena issued forth from the head of Zeus fully armed and equipped, but the votaries of her arts know no such perfection of birth—for them toil ever precedes achievement. So after studying the reliefs diligently, he began to try to copy bits of them, at first probably with no success at all, still he kept on, for he knew there was something to learn from this carving if he could only learn it; and his attempts at imitation grew a little bit like, and then more like, until finally he found he could carve heads quite like those on the sarcophagus if he wanted to, and vary them a bit if he didn't, although if he varied them the faces were still Greek and not Pisan, and they probably looked altogether nicer than the originals because they were not weather-stained or lacking any hands or noses through the mischances of time and travel.

When the Pisans saw what Niccola could do they employed him to make a pulpit for the Baptistery, and this he completed in 1260, being then about 55 years of age. It is perhaps the most beautiful work of its kind in Italy, and has for rival only Niccola's own subsequent work at Siena. It is hexagonal, built entirely of white marble, the angles resting on Corinthian pillars which alternately descend to the ground or are carried on the backs of lions; from their capitals spring trefoiled arches, and above these, on five of the sides of the hexagon, are bas-reliefs of the Nativity, the Adoration of the Kings, the Presentation in the Temple, the Crucifixion, and the Last Judgment.

Dignified in conception, restrained in manner, antique in the stateliness of its beauty, it seems rather the work of one on whose ears echoes of the past have fallen so that he seeks to reawaken and recreate her lost delight, than of one whose work was destined to be a guide and an ensample to future generations; and yet it would be hard to point to any statue or painting executed in the whole extent of Italy, from the Alpine valleys of Piedmont to the sun-steeped plains of Calabria, which can vie with this sculptured pulpit of Niccola Pisano, standing now in the Baptistery of Pisa as it has stood for over six hundred years, in its claim to be considered as the first completed endeavour of renascent Italian art.

For in these bas-reliefs, five years before the birth of Dante, sixteen years before the birth of Giotto, were exemplified the principles which the genius of both was to illustrate,—that the study of the antique was to win back the beauty of its ideal to the service of the present,—that fidelity to nature — the spirits in the Antepurgatory perceiving from Dante's breath that he was alive, gathering round in wonder as the multitude flock round a herald to hear what news he brings : or the hind in the fresco at Assisi, who on hands and knees and with all the eagerness of thirst is drinking the water that springs from the rock: or the goat scratching his ear, in the bas-relief of the Nativity,—that this fidelity to nature, this truth in common things, was as an open sesame to win for the arts entrance in the minds of men, and that the first fruits were dedicate to the service of God.

Comparing Niccola's work with his models, we see that the Phaedra of the sarcophagus has suggested the Madonna in the Adoration of the Kings, and that the high priest in the Presentation is the Bacchus of an antique sculptured vase in the Campo Santo. In these metamorphoses we may see a forecast of how the later exuberance of the quest for beauty was to blend unheedingly things incongruous, — things pertaining to Christ and things pertaining to Diana—grouping reliefs of the story of the Fall and of Hercules and the Centaur around the same baptismal font; and they are a forecast, too, of how, when art was netted in the toils of her own magnificence, and the wings of aspiration no longer strained up to heaven, Phaedra and Bacchus came back as witnesses of her abasement to leer and make revel among the ruins, tempting Josephs and Susannahs on the canvases of Bronzino and Biliverti.

Were it not for the resemblances and for the history attaching to them, we should not perhaps linger long to look at the Greek marbles in Pisa. They would be passed by almost unnoticed among the treasures of the Vatican or the Capitoline; but these for the most part the Roman earth still covered.

Two hundred years and more of unabated effort were to elapse, the impulse given by Niccola Pisano was to animate his successors, and to win new attainment of beauty and truth under Ghiberti and Donatello, and then in the fulness of time, in the dawn of the golden age of the Renaissance, the master works of Greek sculpture which lay buried beneath Rome or in the ruins of the Campagna were uncovered, and to Michael Angelo, studying the Laocoon, the Apollo Belvedere, and the Dying Gladiator, something of their sublime mastery was revealed, even as Niccola Pisano had learnt his simpler lesson from the Phaedra and Hippolytus.

Like spring's first harbingers, which, bursting the sod too early, are nipped by winter's chill, yet in their brief coming are a token and a promise,—so the golden age of Pisa was a precursor of the glory of the Renaissance.

The sceptre of the arts passed from her while her fleets and armies were still potent, and Florence became the heir of her traditions, as at a later period of her sovereignty.

The immediate followers of Niccola Pisano had no succession among her children, and when the structure of the Campo Santo was completed by Giovanni Pisano in 1283 she was constrained to invite artists from Florence and Siena to paint the cloisters in fresco.

In Niccola's pulpit we see the transplanting of the roses of Greek beauty, the establishing of a rose-garden by the banks of the Arno, the fresh green of leaves budding, but it is in Florence that we must seek the second flowering,—the bloom of the perfected rose.

Entering the gallery of the Uffizi, and passing down the Eastern and Southern Corridors amidst Byzantine and Tuscan Madonnas, antique reliefs and busts of Emperors, you reach the hall of Lorenzo Monaco, so named as containing the 'Coronation of the Virgin' of Don Lorenzo, monk of the Camaldoline monastery of the Angeli, and forerunner of Fra Angelico in simplicity and grace.

There are also a tabernacle by Fra Angelico of Madonna and Saints surrounded as by a nimbus by angels playing musical instruments; a panel of saints by Gentile da Fabriano, and a few Quattrocento Florentine pictures, amongst them two by Botticelli,—'The Adoration of the Magi,' and 'The Birth of Venus.' The latter of these let us attempt to consider in detail. It represents Venus rising from the sea off the island of Cythera.

A pale green sea—faintly tremulous with wind-ripples. To the left of the picture, hovering in the air with long wings outspread, are two spirits symbolic of the winds. The cheeks of Eolus are distent, and his breath, visible as a pale shaft of light, is impelling Venus to shore. Her feet are resting on the gold-prank'd edge of a scallop shell, and the waves are dancing before it as it moves onward. She is tall, fair, virginal, undraped, save for the clinging folds of her long, yellow hair. The mythological details might lead us to expect a nymph or nereid,—soulless, elemental, looking out on mankind with something of that expression, half of mockery, half of delight, which Arnold Böcklin's nymphs possess;—but the face is tender and pensive as ever was that of Madonna. But the tenderness of Madonna is tenderness of love revealed, arms encircling the child and eyes lit with the holy light of motherhood, and this is the tenderness of expectancy the tenderness of dawn such as must, have been upon the face of just-awakened Eve,

> 'Beneath her Maker's finger, when the fresh
> First pulse of life shot brightening the snow,'

for Venus, elemental and a goddess, is like Eve coming to earth and vernal delight. It is the garden of earth where she is landing. The receding line of distance where the sea meets the shore is fretted with tiny bays, and verdant with sloping hills. On the right is a laurel grove, and before it a lady, symbolic of Spring, hastens to meet the goddess, holding in outstretched hands a red robe richly enwrought with daisies which gleam upon its folds in white emblazonry. The robe is fluttering in the breath of the wind that wafts the goddess to shore.

In the foreground to the left a few bulrushes are swaying. The stems of the laurels are sparkling with gold, and the sward gleams golden where Venus' feet will tread. Spring is clad in a white robe worked with cornflowers, a spray of olive lies lightly on her breast, and her waist is girdled with roses.

To the left of the picture there are many roses falling. Pale pink roses of hue scarce deeper than the lilied flesh of Venus, some upturned with the heart of the rose laid bare, some the winds have tilted over and they make a Narcissus' mirror of the sea, roses full blown and buds half-opened, they cling to the wings and streaming raiment of the winds, they lie upon their limbs, they flutter softly downwards, they are wafted to the shore, some hurrying joyously, wantonly, some dallying with the ripples of the air. A rain of roses, and the very air that attends their falling seems to murmur of it.

They are the roses of Paestum coming back again; this is the manner of their second flowering. For the delight of the antique world in the presentment of loveliness,—a delight

> 'not yet dead
> But in old marbles ever beautiful'

slept prisoned in marble no longer, but issued forth in newness of life in the Renaissance, and it was in the pictures of Botticelli that it found expression at once most joyous and most complete. Mantegna is indeed in a sense more classical, but in Botticelli this delight is a living reality. For he was the only painter of Italy who, as Ruskin says, 'understood the thoughts of Heathens and Christians equally, and could in a measure paint both Aphrodite and the Madonna.' And understanding the thoughts of both, there is in him no attempt to blend things incongruous. To each their gifts are rendered—unto Caesar and unto God. Myths from Politian by his art made palaces of enchantment of the villas of the Medici, and from Lucian's lines he re-created the 'Calumny' of Apelles. Sixtus IV. sent for him to Rome, and in the Sistine Chapel he painted with Perugino, Pinturicchio, Signorelli, and others of his contemporaries, scenes from the lives of Moses and of Christ.

As all the greatest of artists, alike in painting and in poetry, when of an age he was of his own age,—when local, then of his own city, Florence, — when he needed bystanders, then these, as in the 'Adoration of the Magi,' Florentines,—his contemporaries and himself among them; but the

Madonna of the 'Magnificat' and alike sea-born Venus are neither Jewish nor Greek nor yet Florentine, but timeless according to the measure of his ability to paint the faiths that were in him, and to us in the measure of our faiths—realities.

In the later years of his life he gave up painting Venus and the Spring, and finally gave up the use of the brush altogether, though still for a time, as we shall see, drawing roses. After completing his work in the Sistine Chapel he returned to Florence, and there, says Vasari, 'being whimsical and eccentric, he occupied himself with commenting on a certain part of Dante, illustrating the "Inferno," and executing prints over which he wasted much time, and, neglecting his proper occupation, he did no work, and thereby caused infinite disorder in his affairs. Yet despite Vasari not altogether idle, nor assuredly the less great of spirit in that he thus stood outside his art's achievement and would fain 'put to proof art alien to the artist's' in utterance of his thought. Even so 'Rafael made a century of sonnets,' and 'Dante once prepared to paint an angel.'

His rarer utterance is as theirs extinguished. He was taunted, Vasari tells us, with his unfitness, in that he 'without a grain of learning, scarcely knowing how to read, had undertaken to make a commentary on Dante.' Yet we would gladly, if we could, barter with time the writings of a good many of Dante's commentators in exchange for this same volume.

We are told that he afterwards became one of the followers of Savonarola, and as such totally abandoned the practice of his art and became a Piagnone (a mourning brother), and in his old age in poverty and a cripple he lived on the charity of Lorenzo de' Medici, and of others who had known him in the days of his prosperity.

Time, while robbing us of his commentary on Dante, has dealt with us more kindly as regards the illustrations. They relate not only to the 'Inferno,' as Vasari would lead one to suppose, but to the whole of the 'Divine Comedy' with the exception of a few cantos, and have a unique interest as being the only surviving illustrations of Dante by an artist of the Renaissance. Michael

Angelo is said to have made a similar book of drawings, which was lost at sea in a storm in the Gulf of Lyons.

One of these drawings, seems reminiscent in certain likenesses and contrasts of the picture in the Uffizi.

The subject is Beatrice appearing to Dante in Canto XXX. of the 'Purgatorio.'

Dante and Statius have reached the Terrestrial Paradise, and are walking beside the stream of Lethe conversing with Matelda in the meadow beyond. The mystical Procession of the Church approaching amid the forest heralded by gleaming light and melody has unfolded before them. The triumphal car of the Church drawn by the Gryphon has halted. The twenty-four elders have turned to face it. They are crowned with lilies and are bearing aloft the books of their testimony. One of them, Dante tells us, chants '*Veni Sponsa de Libano*,' and the rest take up the strain, and a hundred angels' voices are heard singing '*Benedictus qui venis*,' and '*Manibus o date lilia plenis*' as they scatter flowers about the car. Behind the elders are the bearers of the seven candlesticks, and the long tongues of flame lie in the air as bands of light, and between them rise the upward sweeping wings of the Gryphon. Around the car the seven virtues are as maidens dancing, and behind it walk seven elders, their temples crowned with roses, among whom walks S. John in the ecstasy of sleep. In the car stands Beatrice,

> 'In white veil with olive wreathed
> A virgin in my view appeared, beneath
> Green mantle, robed in hue of living flame.'

The car is the scallop shell; the elders and the virtues are the attendant spirits, and they too are ministrant upon a lady of love; but her brows are touched by the fadeless olive emblem of wisdom and of peace.

The scallop shell is wafted by the winds to shore, but here the river divides, and it is we who must make the passage. Dante is standing with hands clasped together and eyes downcast. He has looked down in the depths of the river, but from thence his eyes recoil in shame seeing his own image, and seek rather the grasses at his feet; for it is the river of the forgetting of sin, and his eyes are heavy and laden with memories, and cannot as yet endure to meet the vision of the radiance. Beyond the river all around the car, flowers are falling. '*Manibus o date lilia plenis,*'—(scatter ye lilies with hands unsparing)—by a strange but beautiful transition the words uttered by Anchises over the bier of the young Marcellus are sung by angels' voices as they scatter flowers upon the car of Beatrice. Not death this but life, says Botticelli in his drawing, nor alone the pale white of purity, but the fervour of love divine and eternal, and the flowers which the angels are scattering are not lilies alone, but also roses, roses—not of Paestum but of Paradise.

Of the falling roses in the picture in the Uffizi of the 'Birth of Venus' some will flutter to shore, and as they die the seed of beauty will break from the heart of the rose, and the wind will bear it to a soil where it may live. So the roses that were blown to shore on Eolus' breath have given the seeds of many roses; and changed a little by change of environment, they flowered for long in Italy, and some who have visited the garden of their second flowering have gathered the seed and carried it, so that it has flowered in Northern climes and is still flowering. Yet withal, their beauty seems never so supreme as in this the first season of their second flowering in that perfect freshness of the just-awakened rose, and so Botticelli has painted them as spirits in attendance on Love, so that coming to earth she may be reconciled.

The Vita Nuova

IN Boccaccio's life of Dante he says that 'it was customary in Florence, in the spring of the year when the earth was all aflower with beauty, for the citizens to gather together in festival;' and so it happened that on the 1st of May Folco Portinari, a man of considerable position, invited his neighbours to his house to a banquet, and amongst them his neighbour Alighieri, Dante's father, and as even small children accompanied their parents to these festivals Dante went with him, although he was only nine years old. There he met a number of other children of about his own age, and they had the first few courses of the banquet and then played games together. Amongst the others was Folco's daughter Beatrice,—or, as she was always called, Bice—a graceful little child of about eight years old, full of tenderness and winsome ways, perhaps a little more demure and serious in speech than one would have expected at her age: her features were refined and regular: beautiful, but so touched with grace and charm that to many thinking of her it seemed as though she were almost one of the angels.'

'Even so—or how much fairer than I can tell—did she seem to Dante's eyes at this banquet, perhaps not then beheld for the first time, but then first potent to awaken love; and although she was still a child, he took her fair image to his heart with such affection that from that day onwards it never departed all the days of his life.'

In 1373, more than fifty years after Dante's death, the Florentines established a public lectureship on the 'Divina Commedia,' and Boccaccio held the office until his death two years later. His lectures were a commentary on the 'Inferno,' and in a note on the first mention of Beatrice he says—and the statement is confirmed in another commentary supposed to be by Dante's son Pietro: 'This lady, I know from some one in whom I place implicit confidence, who knew her personally, and was in fact a very near relative, was the daughter of the esteemed Folco Portinari. . . . She married a cavalier of the house of Bardi, named Simon, and in the twenty-fourth year of her age she passed from this life, in the year of our Lord 1290.'

These two passages contain all that is known on the subject of Beatrice apart from Dante's own writings; they are the only evidence to connect her with Beatrice Portinari, and they have not been deemed sufficiently conclusive to stay conjecture. Boccaccio did not speak from personal knowledge. He was a child of eight years old at the time of Dante's death. His statements may be accepted with the degree of reservation which always attaches to the utterances of a writer of romance who ventures upon the domain of fact; moreover, as the positive nature of the assurance in the latter passage savours of too much protestation, we may infer from it that a statement in support of which Boccaccio felt it necessary to invoke the authority of a near relative, cannot have been a matter of common knowledge, and consequently that fifty years after Dante's death, when his fame was already so firmly established that his works were the subject of a public lectureship, it was not generally known in Florence who Beatrice was, or whether she had any real existence at all. *Und so weiter!* But enough of these inferences which at most lead but to the land of *Weiss Nicht Wo*, and more probably end only in a state of bemused conjecture as to whether we have arrived there! Boccaccio made a positive statement in a public lecture. He mentioned two families both then prominent in Florence. There is no record of his statement ever having been disputed by them. It is in the highest degree improbable that the statement would have been made unless Boccaccio had been in possession of evidence, or that, if contradicted, the statement should have survived without there being any trace whatsoever of the contradiction. We may assume that what he said was at the time accepted as true by the members of both families, and consequently it is not undue credulity on our part to accept it.

So Beatrice was the daughter of a neighbour of the Alighieri, and Dante saw her when they were both children, and as a child he loved her, and when she grew up to womanhood he loved her, and after her death this love was still for him the greatest of realities. Of his new life as created by this love from the time of his first meeting with Beatrice until about his twenty-seventh year the 'Vita Nuova' tells the story. It ends with a promise; for a new perception born of grieving love is guiding his thoughts upward among untrodden ways, and he has beheld a vision about which he will say nothing until he can discourse more worthily, and his hope is then 'to write concerning her what hath not before been written of any woman.'

The book is the substance of such things as are written in his memory under the rubric '*Incipit Vita Nova*,' and there are collected there sonnets and canzoni, and they are interwoven with an account of the occasion upon which each was written—

the vision of or meeting with Beatrice or his thoughts of her, or self-reproaches, and each poem is followed by an analysis in order that its meaning be more clearly seen; consequently it not infrequently occurs that the same incident is told three times over,—and yet for such reiteration its fervour suffices.

The manner of the telling of the first meeting with Beatrice differs from that of Boccaccio,—no gathering of neighbours and banqueting,—not that these things did not happen, but that it is immaterial whether they happened or no; for we are at once led by the lover into the solitude of love's imaginings. Such facts, however, as recur are not at variance. 'Nine times already since my birth' (I quote here as always from Rossetti's translation) 'had the heaven of light returned to the self-same point almost as concerns its own revolution, when first the glorious Lady of my mind was made manifest to mine eyes. . . . She had already been in this life for so long as that, within her time, the starry heaven had moved towards the Eastern quarter one of the twelve parts of a degree; so that she appeared to me at the beginning of her ninth year almost. . . . At that moment, I say most truly, that the spirit of life, which hath its dwelling in the secretest chamber of the heart, began to tremble so violently that the least pulses of my body shook therewith; and in trembling it said these words: *Ecco Deus fortior me, qui veniens dominabitur mihi.*'

From that time forward Love governed his soul. Nine years later he met Beatrice walking with two ladies, and she saluted him. After this there appeared to him a vision—the figure of a lord of terrible aspect holding in his arms a lady sleeping, and showing him a heart burning in flames, and saying '*Vide cor tuum,*'—and making a sonnet concerning this vision he sent it to his friends, and they in sonnets conjectured as to its meaning, but perceived it not. Given up now wholly to thinking of Beatrice, the timidity of his love made him conceal from all, by whose help it was that love had gained this mastery over him; and once as he sat watching Beatrice in church, a lady who was sitting in a direct line between them looked at him many times, for it seemed as though upon her his glances were fixed, and so his friends perceiving this deemed that this was the lady who had brought him to such a pass of love. Dante, hearing this, was reassured that his secret had not become known, and wrote rhymes in honour of this lady that so she might be a screen for his love. After she had left the city Love came to him in a vision in the light habit of a traveller, and bade him take another lady to be a screen for his love for Beatrice, that it might not be revealed. This he did with such success that many talked of it, and Beatrice heard of it, and on meeting him in the street passed by without greeting him. Then being for the first time denied her salutation, he was filled with such grief that he wept and prayed in his chamber in solitude, and there suddenly falling asleep like a beaten sobbing child, again Love came to him in a vision and bade him tell her all things in a poem, and how he had been hers even from childhood, and to have the words fitted with a pleasant music and played where she might chance to hear them, and into the music Love himself would pass whensoever it was needful. He awoke and wrote as Love had bidden him, with what issue may be inferred from the fact that one of the thoughts which then troubled him was that 'the lady whom Love hath chosen out to govern me, is not as other ladies whose hearts are easily moved.' After this it chanced that a friend took him to a gathering of ladies among whom was Beatrice, and he found on arriving that it was a wedding, and he was persuaded to stay, but being seized with faintness and trembling leant against a picture in the room; and there raising his eyes he saw Beatrice, and was filled with such confusion that she and her friends whispered of it to each other, and it seemed that they mocked him. He went away sorrowfully, and in his solitude tried to express in verse which might come into her hearing why it was that he was dumb and confused in her sight, and why, although a mark for scorn when in her company, he yet sought to behold her.

After this the secret of his heart being understood of many, he was one day asked by certain ladies, 'To what end lovest thou this lady, seeing that thou canst not support her presence?' And he told them that the end and aim of his love was but the salutation of that lady, wherein he found that beatitude which was the goal of desire.

The thought came to him that some day Beatrice would die. To realize this was to suffer the bitterness of death. In phantasy he beheld a throng of ladies who went hither and thither, weeping, and the sun went out so that the stars showed themselves, and they were of such a colour that he knew they must be weeping; and it seemed that the birds fell dead out of the sky, and there were great earthquakes. And looking towards Heaven he beheld a multitude of angels returning upwards singing '*Osanna in Excelsis*,' and it seemed that he went to look upon the body wherein her spirit had had its abiding place, and that he beheld Beatrice in death. Certain ladies seemed to be covering her head with a white veil, and she was so humble of aspect that it was as though she had said, 'I have attained to look on the beginning of peace'; and he cried out to Death, 'Now come unto me, and be not bitter against me any longer: surely where thou hast been thou hast learnt gentleness. Wherefore come now unto me who do greatly desire thee.'

The phantasy so possessed him that he cried aloud on Death, so that certain ladies hearing his cry came and wakened him, and tried to comfort him. The phantasy was presage of fact which soon followed it. Once more he met Beatrice. He was full of gladness and we may infer that she saluted him; and then one day as he sat trying to express in verse what indeed her influence on him was, the news came of her death;—

'The Lord God of Justice called my most excellent lady unto Himself, that she might be glorious under the banner of that blessed Queen Mary whose name had always a deep reverence in the words of holy Beatrice.'

To speak of the manner of her departure

is not necessary, nor would his pen suffice to do it fitly, and he would then be constrained to say somewhat in his own praise; but he tells how after that his eyes were so weary of weeping that he could no longer thereby give ease to sorrow, he bethought him of a few words of lamentation to stand him in stead of tears, and herein speaks of her; for

'Beatrice is gone up into high Heaven,
The kingdom where the angels are at peace;
And lives with them: and to her friends is dead;'

and he wrote a second time in her memory at the request of one of her kinsmen, who came asking him to write something on a lady who had died, but feigning to speak of some other lady; and Dante perceiving that he spoke of Beatrice gave utterance to his own grief in such words as might be spoken by her kinsman.

On the anniversary of her death, filled with the remembrance of her, he sat drawing the figure of an angel upon certain tablets, and so sitting, becoming sorrowful and changing countenance, and then being in dread lest any one had seen him, he raised his eyes and saw a lady young and beautiful looking down with pity upon him from a window; and seeing her pity, his eyes were the more inclined to tears, so that he withdrew from her sight. But whenever the lady saw him afterwards she became pale and of a piteous countenance, as though she had been in love, reminding him indeed of Beatrice, who was wont to be of a like pallor. And he began to be gladdened by the constant sight of this lady, and then had unrest and rebuked himself, cursing the unsteadfastness of his eyes, in that they had forgotten their condition of weeping, at the glance of a lady who had merely had compassion for the grief they had shown for his own blessed lady. And then he began to consider that this lady was young and beautiful, and gentle, and that it was perhaps Love himself who had set her in his path that his life might find peace. While thus wavering he saw in phantasy Beatrice appearing as a child, clad in the crimson raiment she had worn when he had first seen her, and then his memory began to recall one by one all the occasions on which he had met her, and his heart repented of its wandering desire, and from that hour he thought constantly of Beatrice in humility and shame. The lady at the window, gentle and full of pity, has been supposed to be Gemma Donati, whom he married about a year after the death of Beatrice, or to be a personification of philosophy, wherein he sought, and to some extent found, consolation, or to refer to some lady otherwise unknown, and Dante in mentioning her has not shrunk from the recording of some wandering fancy and the subsequent bitterness of remorse.

This much is common to conjecture, that at some period after the death of Beatrice he wavered in the constancy of his love, that then the cloud that had veiled her image from his sight was dispelled, and his thoughts were ever fixed upon her in humility. She who in life had been to him almost as a spirit, became something more; 'a new perception born of grieving love' guided his thought upward, and of this he will write further.

It is one of the earliest, and it shares with 'Aucassin and Nicolete' the claim to be regarded as the tenderest love-story in mediaeval literature. But by contrast how virile the song story, how dreamlike the book of the new life! For in 'Aucassin and Nicolete,' the minstrel sings of the love that 'many waters cannot quench,' love more potent than desire to be dubbed knight or follow tourneys, more potent too than 'threats of hell and hopes of paradise,' enduring captivity and the fear of death, fleeing from the castle to a lodge of boughs in the meadows, and ending in happiness 'by God's will who loveth lovers.'

In the 'Vita Nuova' the lover is pale and protesting, prone alike to verse and tears, to hold colloquies with love, and to call on passers-by for pity, but shrinking from rather than seeking contact with the lady; and the lady—she is gentle, pitiful, but yet a shadow, —she glides silently across our path of vision, she is robed in red or in white, she is attended by one or more other ladies;—a word, a gentle look, and she has passed by, and we only see the lover repining in solitude, or writing verses to other ladies in order to veil the identity of his love.

Dreamlike and fantastic, it seems a scene from some faded arras, fresh and lifelike only in its dim-lit corridor, where all colour is attuned, and where the sun is a thing forgotten,—a pageant in some Provençal Court of Love, and this the mask of love unattainable, although by the rules of the Court the verses ought to move pity and something more.

Dreamlike and mystic, hard to translate to a world of human endeavour and human love, and the sense of this may in some degree lend weight to the supposition that Beatrice is from the first only a symbol,—a symbol of divine philosophy,—that Dante was not in love with flesh and blood at all, that he was either a dreamer in love with dreams, or a scholar in love with knowledge, turning aside from the divine to the pride of the knowledge of the earth, and then groping his way back in abasement. Such supposition, however, Dante's own testimony overrides. Love-language is not used by him in metaphor. When he wrote of love he was of love inspired; witness his reply to the question put to him in Purgatory by Bonagiunta of Lucca:—

> 'But say if here his face I scan
> Who those new rimes drew forth, that ran,
> "Ye ladies in whose sense
> Is love's intelligence?"
> I answered, "I am one who hark
> To love's inspiring, and I mark
> As he within doth teach
> To utter forth my speech."'[1]

And Bonagiunta confessed that for this reason Dante's love-poems had surpassed his own and those of Jacopo da Lentino and Guittone d'Arezzo, for they had often feigned the love they wrote of.

This is explete and positive. Love in the 'Vita Nuova' is not a synonym or symbol, but a reality;—dreamlike, ethereal, ever fluttering on visionary wings,—but so far a reality as to find a temporary casement in flesh and blood,—'seeking in a mortal image the likeness of what is perhaps eternal.' Such then as he has portrayed was Dante in his new life.

[1] 'Purgatorio,' XXIV. 49 *seq.* (Shadwell's Trans.).

This lover, tearful and shrinking, hardly tallies with the picture which contemporary records would lead us to form of Dante during his life in Florence. It need not tally :—

> 'God be thanked, the meanest of his creatures
> Boasts two soul-sides, one to face the world with,
> One to show a woman when he loves her !'

And the soul-side revealed in the 'Vita Nuova' is not that that faced the world.

For he did face the world; he was no recluse who would fain flee from life's turmoil; a student too proud and reserved for popularity, he was one of the leading Florentine poets, the friend as such of Guido Cavalcanti and Cino da Pistoia ; the singer of the charms of the sixty fairest ladies in Florence in a *serventese*,—and to compile such a list was only possible for one who to some extent had mingled in social pleasures. There is evidence tending to show that he had already visited Paris, that he had studied at Padua and Bologna, that he had taken part in the victory of the Guelphs over the Ghibellines at the battle of Campaldino. He had married Gemma Donati, a member of a prominent Florentine family. He had begun to take a part in public affairs. His name appears in 1299 as one of an embassy to S. Gemignano, and in the following year he was appointed one of the priors of the city. Life was opening before him varied fields of activity and honourable service. Suddenly this prospect was dispelled. The Guelphs had been rent into the factions of the Whites and Blacks. The latter, in alliance with the Papacy, brought Charles of Valois to Florence, and in 1301 the leaders of the Whites were banished, among them being Dante.

His exile was lifelong. Twenty years of wandering to and fro over Italy. Welcomed and tarrying for a time at some noble's court —the Scalas or the Polentas—but learning

> 'come sa di sale
> Lo pane altrui, e com'è duro calle
> Lo scendere e'l salir per l'altrui scale.'

Wandering to and fro, all cities open to him except Florence, to be burnt if he returns there. Hoping for a time for recall through a change in government, and then wearying of the futile plots and hopes of exiles and the perpetual strife of factions, seeing peace and prosperity for Italy only in the vision of the coming of a ruler who should heal all factions—and this a dim, dim vision.

The soul-side that faced the world grew grim and furrowed; his letters on public affairs are filled with bitterness and indignation.

And what of the other soul-side?—that revealed in the 'Vita Nuova,' and as yet revealed there only—scarce known to Beatrice in life, timorous in her presence, silent from a sense of the sanctity of love, eloquent only in solitude. It is still turned towards her and to the regions where she dwells,—turned more openly, for there is no fear now that she will misconceive. Turned more steadfastly, thanks to Florence and her sentence of banishment; and the city claims our gratitude in that she thus dealt unjustly, and like wisdom she is of her children justified, for the path to life's achievement for the many is civic contentment, but not for the writer of the 'Divine Comedy.'

Thus turned steadfastly to her image, he makes his own soul pilgrimage from sight to insight. Still bitter the manner of the losing,—and yet what a Barmecide's feast this—these factions, this Florence, transient and lost by exile—in contrast with that new life which awoke within him in boyhood at sight of Beatrice, the life which time and exile changed not, only established! Dreamlike and fantastic in utterance, but it is the utterance of the ideal, of the imperishable, of the eternal element in mutable things,

> 'For life with all its yield of joy and woe,
> Of hope and fear,
> Is just our chance of the prize of learning love,
> How love hath been, may be indeed, and is.'

Beatrice dead—his thoughts are linked with the unseen, his life is a witness of her memory. After that, being led in vision through hell and purgatory, he has attained to her presence, her memory is lost in what that memory has revealed—in the radiance which is about the throne.

In contrast with other records of mediaeval

love the 'Vita Nuova' seems at once more mystic and more personal.

Every singer sang of love, of the praise of some lady from whose eyes arrows were flying—arrows of disdain piercing as serpent's tooth, and arrows of tenderness and pity that on a sudden transfixed the heart with imperishable hope,—and they sang alike her cruelty and her grace, and how she alone could heal the wounds that she imparted.

The love whereof they sang varied with the singer. It was Platonic or of a more earthly essence; it was romantic or homely.

Cecco loved Becchina and sang how, when he saw her in a rage, he stood like a little trembling lad.

Jaufre Rudel sang his love for the Countess of Tripoli, never indeed having seen her, hearing only of her virtues from pilgrims coming from the East, and his life is the greatest of his poems:—

'There lived a singer in France of old,
By the tideless, dolorous, midland sea,
In a land of sand, and ruin, and gold,
There shone one woman and none but she;

And, finding life for her love's sake fail,
Being fain to see her, he bade set sail,
Touched land, and saw her as life grew cold,
And praised God, seeing; and so died he.'

Selvaggia, Fiammetta, Joan—they live in the pages of their poets; a shadowy existence, yet as shadows they are beautiful and the laments for their deaths speak a reality of sorrow. Singer and ladies—they are a part of the masque of mediaevalism.

A distinctive, we may almost say a dominating feature of that pre-Renaissance life,—severing it alike from the life of the ages preceding and following—is the reverence shown to woman, at times a worship half idolatrous, at times the pursuit of a distant ideal. The singer sang of the lady; the knight fought for her; the supreme aim of each was to be thought worthy in her sight, to live and die in her service. This reverence was in origin religious. The Madonna had imparted something of her mystic purity to all her sex. She was enthroned above all saints and kings, and something of her glory was reflected upon all womanhood, and the lover's privilege was service.

The history of mediaeval love is a record of the deviations from this ideal, but in tracing them the ideal is still perceptible. Love might be, often was, in essence a transgression against honour and faith,—yet even as such it had whatever palliation may spring from the fact that it was abiding, 'that it changed not for weal or woe all the days of their life.'

Devotion to his lady was the duty of every knight of the Round Table, and yet in considering the book of their deeds we are minded of the message of La Beale Isoud to the Queen ;—'that there be within the land but four lovers, that is Sir Launcelot du Lake and queen Guenever and Sir Tristram de Liones and queen Isoud ;' and as in contrast with these two histories other records of knightly love are dimmed in lustre, so of all the loves which found utterance in song four names find imperishable testimony—Dante and Beatrice, and Petrarch and Laura.

Much more of Laura is revealed in Petrarch's sonnets than Dante ever reveals of Beatrice. We may picture her—fair, tall, flaxen-haired, gentle and comely as is the figure in Simon Memmi's fresco in the Spanish Chapel at Florence, which Vasari says to be Madonna Laura,—and the lover's long devotion must touch with sympathy and interest, and the beauty of the presentment is a charm perennial.

The sonnets are the work of Petrarch's mature age, and in contrasting them with the 'Vita Nuova' we are contrasting strength with immaturity, the chiselled, flawless grace of lyric adoration and regret of the scholar and diplomat with the timorous imaginings and self-communings of youth.

Yet for this reason, for this reticence, the 'Vita Nuova' is at once more mystic and more personal.

The love is a reality—and yet this vision dimly seen, this embodiment of the whisperings of hope, is not mediaeval—is not Florentine. It is unfettered by age or habitation.

We know that Laura died five hundred years ago and more, although her name lives on the living lips of her poet; of this vision something lives other than the memory something that gathers to itself the dreams of whoso reads it, and touches and transfigures them into new and fairer semblance, and is in turn by them transfigured and puts on new name and lineage.

The love that here found language was a love which gave all and asked for nothing,—nothing save only her salutation,—a love supreme alike in passion and in purity.

Palmers, Pilgrims, and Romers

BY a certain innate faculty of symbolism, colours are suggestive of conditions or qualities. Violet has been said by Mendelssohn to be the supreme colour of music—as being the faint hue which the air takes in vibrating to its harmony; and the first violet, legend tells, was born of melody, for it grew on the spot of earth where the lyre of Orpheus rested when he fell asleep after playing to the woods and mountains. Red is the colour of love; green is at times a pledge of hope or peace—at times, witness of envy; white is the emblem of purity. Such symbolism is, for the most part, of general acceptance, and the connection of thought is either instinctive, or, when realized, is abiding. Certain colours may, however, have for each of us a several and distinct sphere of suggestion. Some particular hue when it meets the eye has the power to touch certain chords of memory so that it speaks from the past, recalling the associations of some place visited, or awakening some mood of thought.

In certain of the French and Italian cathedrals, wandering amid the grey light of nave and transept, you may see some window suffused with a rich warmth of colour. It will probably be one of the older windows —fourteenth or fifteenth century at latest— and the colour of the glass is richer and softer than that of any in the windows more recent. The subject represented there—a scene from the life of Christ or from the Old Testament—is perhaps indistinct and not easily recognisable. The blue and purple of the raiments are darkened and scarce distinguishable from the silt left by rain and wind without and the dust of centuries within. But while blackening the darker colours the lapse of time has mellowed and deepened those that are paler, blending them in a soft rich harmony of rose and yellow, so that whether the window face east or west, whether it be in choir, aisle, or transept, it would seem all day long as though the sky beyond it were glowing with sunlight, and that the window but catches and transmits its radiance—red as gold and pale as amber flame.

This glow of soft light of early stained-glass is one of art's lost secrets, and like the Cathedrals Gothic or Romanesque wherein we find it, is at once a peculiar creation and testimony of the Mediaeval Age, and looking upon it in lifted window of quiet fane, the gleam of colour becomes a symbol, for it seems to enshrine something of the fervour of mediaeval faith.

Of some of the characteristics of this faith and of its fervour let us attempt to consider.

In this quest,—in attempting to touch with words 'the substance of things hoped for, the evidence of things not seen,' one must needs walk humbly, and gladly at times tread in worn footsteps.

'Before the twelfth century the nations were too savage to be Christian, and after the fifteenth too carnal to be Christian.' Let us assume that in the Mediaeval Age men were neither pre-eminently savage, nor pre-eminently carnal, or—as in the form of the sentence I have quoted from 'Val d'Arno' the last epithet applies to our own age—we may perhaps soften it into saying that they were not pre-eminently luxurious or occupied with material interests. We are not as yet much nearer to seeing what the condition of this Mediaeval Age was, only we have agreed that it was neither of these two conditions of barbarism or luxury—either of which was incompatible with fervour of faith. The one state had not yet arisen, the other had passed away, and in passing left the condition of the western nations a peculiarly receptive one, and tidings of things unseen fell upon willing ears. The more primitive is man's condition, the more human effort is, perforce, spent in immediate contact with nature, and the more the instinct is susceptible to its influence.

In the earliest literature of the dwellers on the western sea-board, the influence of natural environments is seen to have certain common characteristics,—the more apparent when the more remote and exempt from rival influences of Central and Southern Europe. The Celts faced the expanse of an unknown sea, and the Atlantic was to them ever a nurse of the imagination. When the sea rose up to the sky-line, calm and peaceful, the track of the sunlight seemed a pathway over the waves to some other world of tradition. When the sea rose up to the sky-line in the fierce fury of tempest, the beating of the surf and the crying of the wind were alike voices from the unknown. With scents of the unknown the wind was laden, and when the mist veiled the grey sky and lay thick upon the shore, the unknown came nearer. So the Atlantic became a supreme teller of stories, and such as heard them tried to sing them again to their fellows, and their utterance was mystic and dreamlike, and as a broken fragment, for something in the voices of the sea had eluded memory, and they strove in vain to recapture it. Christianity radiating from Rome, touched the sea-board and the western isles—coming neither iconoclastic nor protesting—not to destroy but to fulfil.

The Atlantic was still a mother of inspiration—a supreme teller of stories—but her whisperings of the infinite were touched with new meaning, and of the union 'du naturalisme celtique avec le spiritualisme chrétien' came the imaginative fervour of early Celtic idealism.

More than ever now in vision wanderers, they seek not the fulfilment of the hopes of things material, but the complete attainment of their renunciation. The isle of the amorous queens had awaited the coming of Bran the son of Febal,—the joys of combat had alternated with the joys of love, as incentives for the earlier voyagers—but now the bourn of endeavour has changed—the voyagers find islands where hermits dwell in solitude, and birds bring food for them, islands where the birds sing canticles daily at matins, lauds, and prime, and as they travel they make fastings and prayers, and they come at last to the earthly paradise.

This idealism—mystic yet adventurous—

found in some measure in the earlier writings of all Celtic nations, reached supreme beauty of utterance in Ireland; there growing in isolation and without influence on the rest of Europe until after the landing of the Normans in Britain. The conquerors were subdued by its beauty, and in great measure assimilating its spirit they retold the legends of the voyages and visions of S. Brendan, S. Patrick, Tundal and others in their own language,—and so France was in turn invaded by Celtic poetry. There had entered also another stream of influence coming from the East—I cannot say how or when it entered—but the life of S. Alexis, which dates from the eleventh century, and which is the earliest surviving work of any magnitude and literary value written in mediaeval French, is charged with marks of eastern origin.

The difference between these two streams of influence—the early mystic idealisms of the West and of the East—is the difference of natural environment. The quickenings of thought in solitude by the western ocean are imaginative and adventurous—dreams of unknown worlds, visions of hell, and hopes of paradise. The ocean of the eastern mystic is the wilderness—not unknown—the wilderness where Christ had fasted for forty days, and where the Devil had been empowered to tempt him; and so the quickenings of thought of those who fled from the world to dwell in the deserts of Syria and Egypt were not imaginative but ascetic. They knew what lay in wait in the solitude. They were going as outposts in the country of the great enemy to wrestle with the principle of sin. The contest would be lifelong,—ever warring against sedition within the citadel of the flesh, and attacks from evil from without,—and the weapons of their faith were scourgings, fastings, and prayer.

The excesses of the ascetics are a strange chapter in the history of fanaticism. Pitiful self-torture—this constant warfare of sense and spirit, men dwelling as beasts in caves, naked—treating their humanity as a vile thing to be scourged into submission to hunger and cold. So rigorous was the regimen that often reason failed—

and hence the eastern reverence for the insane.

The fairer side of ascetic life, and some of its shadow, may be seen reproduced in Pietro Lorenzetti's fresco of the 'Hermits of the Thebaid' in the Campo Santo at Pisa. There, for the most part, they are reading or meditating, or are engaged in rural pursuits. There are also incidents from the lives of certain of the hermits—the temptation of S. Anthony, and Christ appearing to him in vision, S. Hilarion subduing a dragon by the sign of the Cross, and the visit of S. Anthony to S. Paul, the patriarch of the hermits, who had dwelt in the wilderness for over ninety years.

In the life by S. Jerome, the old hermit says to S. Anthony: 'Thou beholdest me still alive indeed, but about to become dust. Yet since love sustains the universe, tell me, I beseech you, how it fares with the human race,—whether new buildings are rising in old cities, under whose empire the world is now governed, and whether any survive of those who were deluded by the error of devils?'

The exquisite humanity and tenderness of this may perhaps be weighed against some of the grosser realities of demoniacal torment and the posturings of S. Simeon Stylites, and asceticism not be judged entirely by its excesses.

In the adjacent fresco of the 'Triumph of Death' the contrast between the contemplative life of the hermits and that of worldly vanity is vividly shown in the figure of S. Macarius who stands before a party of knights and ladies who are riding back from the chase, and points them to three open coffins. The horses' nostrils are dilated with fear, one lady seems touched with pity, Uguccione is holding his nose at the sight, and the cavalcade rides on unheedingly.

Perhaps the earliest instance of the influence of this eastern asceticism in the national as apart from the devotional literature of western Europe is the French poem on the life of S. Alexis written in the eleventh century. The details are softened, but the principles are unchanged. It tells how Alexis, the only son of Euphemian, a rich Roman lord, leaves his father's house on the evening of his marriage, bidding his wife take Christ alone for her husband, for in this world there is no perfect love, and all joy is turned to sorrow; and how he goes to Edessa, gives away all the money he has and lives as a beggar, and as such is given alms by two of his father's servants who have been sent to seek him. After seventeen years he returns to Rome, and meeting his father, appeals to him for succour in the name of his lost son, and is allowed to sit beneath the steps of his palace. There he remains for seventeen years, fed on the waste from his father's table, a mark for the rough jests of his slaves, daily seeing his wife and parents enter and depart, and hearing them weep because of his absence. At last, when dying, he asks for writing materials to be brought to him, and writes the story of his life. Meanwhile a miraculous voice is heard in the city bidding men seek the man of God who is in the house of Euphemian; and the Pope and a great multitude come, and the scroll is taken from the hand of the beggar as he dies, and then all know his history and honour him as a saint. The church of S. Alessio now covers the spot where the palace stood, and the staircase is still preserved as a holy relic.

Against the cruelty involved in this ideal of the renunciation of all earthly happiness, the humanity of the poet breaks out in protest in the reproaches which the parents utter when they learn that the son whose absence they have mourned is the dead beggar at their gate. Euphemian, lamenting that he is left childless, bewailing his own blindness in not recognising his son, admits his sanctity and self-sacrifice, yet exclaims: 'Helmet and hauberk thou shouldst have worn, and been girt with the sword as were thy equals: thine it was to govern well thy mighty retinue, and to bear the emperor's standard even as did I and thy ancestors.' The mother, kissing and embracing the body, asks him why he has had no pity for them, why he has never spoken to her if only once; and his wife joining her tears to theirs, contrasts the emaciated form with the youthful beauty of the husband she had loved.

The poet's protest is more than the mourners' utterance of grief, for the faith of Alexis is not only pitiless but sterile, and the ideal of eastern asceticism failed to satisfy the dawning conception of mediaeval Christianity.

II

Before the twelfth century the nations were too savage to be Christian;—something of the savage in the ascetic; and in the Celtic vista more of the unknown of terror than of joy;—visions of hell and reality of torments in Dante's precursors, but only searchings for paradise. These two streams of influence—the mystic idealism of the West, the mystic asceticism of the East—each born of the communings of faith with nature—with the ocean and the wilderness—were perfected in union. In the life-endeavour of those whose memory makes mediaeval faith seem to us fervid, these two principles are underlying—the fleeing to the wilderness, the renunciation of earthly self-seeking,—and the voices of the western wonder-world calling not to tarry, but to go forth into the unknown,—to win the Holy Graal, to win paradise—rousing the soul thus purified by renunciation to an ecstasy of effort. 'And they confessed that they were strangers and pilgrims on the earth, and they wandered to and fro in pilgrimage': — palmers, pilgrims, and romers. For, as Dante says in the 'Vita Nuova'—(I quote from Rossetti's translation),—'there are three separate denominations proper unto those who undertake journeys to the glory of God. They are called Palmers who go beyond the seas eastward, whence often they bring palm-branches; and Pilgrims are they who journey unto the holy House of Galicia; seeing that no other apostle was buried so far from his birthplace as was the blessed Saint James. And there is a third sort who are called Romers; in that they go unto Rome.' As pilgrims they would fain win pardon for sin by prayer in some shrine sacred with the memory of saints; and they told strange stories when they returned from wandering, for the world seemed to them a thing mysterious. The Dark Ages were over, and their eyes were indeed fixed on the Light; but the darkness was not so long passed by as that shadows had lost their terror, and as they wandered the enchantments of evil were manifest to them and perils lay in wait about their path. Yet must there be earnest of their faith other than pilgrimage and prayer. Renunciation —yes, and something other than this; for although strangers they are here for a purpose, and they must be doing while they wait, and leave something behind them that shall testify. As yet no continuing city—but in the cities of their tarrying they build temples of praise, and the arts are the handmaids of faith to do her purposes and make beautiful her dwelling-places. Write, build, paint, fight—they must do something, however visionary, if only the endeavour be o the glory of God; retire apart from the world may be, and as at Alvernia and Clairvaux make the wilderness fertile in His praise; but not sit beneath the steps as a beggar if the brain have purpose or the hand have strength. For 'the two arms wherewith we ought to embrace God are firm faith and good works; both are necessary if we would hold fast unto God, for the one without the other is worth nothing.' This is a part of the *Credo* of the Sire de Joinville the Seneschal, who went crusading with S. Louis and wrote his biography.

So the fervour of faith becomes action, and, girt still in mystic garment, she walks upon the earth, and her footprints are visible. The saints of this age are no longer for us types, myths or abstractions, but men and women who led holy lives. We may indeed consider as the day-dream of a monk's fantasy the legend of S. Ursula, the daughter of King Maurus, sailing over the sea in pilgrimage with her eleven thousand maidens and suffering martyrdom at Cologne, and deem that the princess never had life other than that she has to-day in the pictures of Carpaccio and Hans Memling; we may consider the legend of S. Barbara shut in a tower by her father that she might not be seen of men, to be a re-telling of the story of Danae and of the vain attempt of King Acrisius to avert the decree of the Gods; and disbelieving now in dragons, S. George—being left as a hero without an antagonist—may be relegated with the princess Cleodolinda to the domain of mythology as a variant of Perseus and Andromeda; but however rationalistic our point of view, we can hardly doubt the reality of the existence of S. Catherine of Siena, or of her interview with Gregory VI., and the return of the Papal court from Avignon; or that Jeanne, the village maiden of Domrémy, thought she heard a voice from heaven telling her that her king should be crowned in Rouen, and the English should be driven back, and that she followed the thought or the voice—which you will—and the king won back his kingdom; or that S. Louis, ninth king of France of that name, went crusading. The imaginative piety potent in literature becomes potent in life—and they who are touched by it in spirit, dead to the world, are yet in it a mighty moving force.

The mystic ideals of the Celt and of the hermit are seen transfigured by a new love of humanity in the ideals of court and cloister. It is in the pages of their earliest biographers that we may best learn something of the spirit of those whose lives were of these ideals the highest measure of attainment; for they in writing of them are uncritical, expect not questioning, are neither apologetic to disarm it or circumstantial to confute, being touched in some measure with the same simple and childlike faith. So instancing S. Francis of Assisi as type of the monastic ideal 'arising as a sun upon the world' we must look to the life by S. Bonaventura, who as a child had been healed by him, or to the scenes from this life painted by Giotto in the Upper Church at Assisi, or to the Fioretti—'the flowers, miracles and devout examples' of S. Francis and his followers. Yet the extreme sanctity of S. Francis had so impressed itself upon his contemporaries that he moved as a saint among men, and as such, filled with love for all men and all created things, he appears in the pages of his earliest biographers. Of no age, of no group of his contemporaries can it be claimed that of them he was typical.

As type of the monastic ideal choosing retirement in order the more completely to consecrate the talents to the service of God, we may instance Fra Angelico; and his life—gentle, spiritual, imaginative,—may be seen mirrored in his art in tabernacle and altar-piece and in the frescoes in the cells of the convent of S. Marco; and for other proof of the holiness whereby he came to be named of the angels which he painted, we may read in the life by Vasari: 'He laboured continually at his paintings, but would do nothing that was not connected with things holy. He might have been rich, but for riches he took no care; on the contrary he was accustomed to say that the only true riches was contentment with little. . . . In fine, this never sufficiently to be lauded father was most humble, modest and excellent in all his words and works; in his painting he gave evidence of piety and devotion, as well as of ability, and the saints that he painted have more of the air and expression of sanctity than have those of any other master.'

In the Mediaeval Age the realization of the monastic ideal attained to the extreme of sanctity; and yet it belongs to it less exclusively than does the ideal chivalrous. The monk's faith is ever apt to seem rather a thing apart from his age than a witness of it. Love divine and love human have been planted together in the hearts of men, and they were marrying and giving in marriage and the immortal tenderness of human relationship was ever recurrent, and they were wandering to and fro over the earth and fighting and trading and marking out kingdoms; and some taking their share in all this, yet follow the spirit of an inner dream, and to its bidding they are ministrant, and it tells them that nothing that is pure is too lowly to be done or too great to be attempted, and walking in its guidance they are in the forefront of endeavour. To some it will appear that they can more truly serve their purpose in the cloister than in the world, and by the fact of this withdrawal from life's turmoil, they cannot of their age be typical, and that they seem to be not at variance with it is witness of the faith of their fellows.

The type of mediaeval imaginative piety is not monastic—is neither the saint in poverty, nor the monk in his cloister, but rather the knight-errant riding forth to meet adventure in the name of God and his lady.

The Celtic restlessness is thus transformed into a rule of conduct. The knight's vow is as much a consecration as the vow of priesthood, and the quest on which he enters is lifelong: to succour the weak, to war against wrong and unfaith. Many adventures lay about his path, and the sword never rusted in the scabbard. It was an age of conflict—much of it against unfaith, notably in Spain and Sicily; for there the knight might win fame akin to that of the Paladins of history and romance, who had fought at Roncesvalles and Aliscans.

The whole literature of chivalry,—the *chansons de geste*, the legends of Arthur, alike full of the memory of heroic deeds,—

had been a call to action; and the appeal of Urban II. at the Council of Clermont fell upon eager ears. There should be no peace while Christ's sepulchre was in the hands of the Saracens. He came not to send peace until all things were fulfilled. The host of warrior pilgrims depart, and most of them return no more. But for nigh two hundred years the call is on occasion heard again. Votary succeeds to votary, S. Bernard to Peter the Hermit. Dead are those who had preached before and those who went crusading, and their conquests—if haply they conquered aught—are lost; still the same response is made, private feuds are abandoned, and the host sets out to recover the Holy Sepulchre, and S. Bernard tears his robe in pieces to make crosses for his hearers, and the wave of the knighthood of Christendom foams itself away upon the shore of Syria or of Egypt, or is spent in foam before ever it reaches the soil of the unbeliever. In the chronicling of the quest we may see the fervour of the knight's imaginings, and the falterings of his footsteps and his purpose, for this quest is for the knights of Christendom even as that of the San Graal for the knights of Arthur's Round Table, in that it cannot be achieved by prowess in arms alone.

Alike in a measure is the manner of the avowing of the quest—the vision splendid of endeavour beckoning the assembly at Clermont forth from their accustomed selves, and the mystic vision apparent to the knights at Camelot. As they sat at meat together there entered within the hall the Holy Graal covered with white samite, but none might see it nor who bear it, and when it had been borne through the hall, then the holy vessel departed suddenly so that they wist not whither. The crying of thunder and a radiant light had heralded its coming, and all in silence had looked each at other, and each in this light had seemed fairer than ever before. And after its departing they had found speech, and Sir Gawaine first and then the rest had made a vow that on the morrow without longer abiding, they would labour in the quest of the San Graal for a year and a day or more if need be, and that they would return again no more to the Court until they had seen it more openly.

So they set out on their quest: but to the holy knights alone success was given, and two of these were buried in the city of Sarras, and Sir Bors alone returned to tell of it. The others—Sir Launcelot, 'that had no peer of any earthly sinful man,'—Sir Gawaine and the rest—their travail availed not.

We are considering an historical event and the memory of the lives of men, and we have no wish to idealize the scene; yet it is only thus in legend that we can parallel the imaginative ecstasy of the invocation and response of Christian chivalry, and each man as he took the cross must have seemed to his fellows as seemed the knights at Camelot, 'fairer than ever before.' The ecstasy is of the inception of purpose. As the knights of the San Graal digressed, and the memory of old deeds and old desires was still potent,—so also the knights Crusaders. 'Whoever,' was the decree, 'through devotion, and neither to gain honours nor wealth, shall set out for Jerusalem to deliver the Holy Sepulchre, his journey shall be counted to him for full penance'; and there were few if any who after the journey's ending must look not still to win pardon of mercy, and not as due. Not many for long served God for nought. In the first Crusade Jerusalem was captured, and Godfrey was made Defender of the Holy Sepulchre, refusing to wear a kingly crown in the city where Christ had worn a crown of thorns; and then many deeming that the quest was ended returned to their own lands, taking no thought for the maintaining of what they had won; and others remained to found kingdoms and principalities, and they had forgotten their vow and were at variance, and fell before the Saracens.

Their successors never reached the holy city. Much digression of purpose, and for the most part voluntary,—but Venetians must be paid for their ferrying—Shylocks to their bond—and with result for them more prosperous. Although incidentally there was shedding of Christian blood at

Zara, and more later on at Constantinople, and the conquest for a time of the Byzantine Empire,—with result to weaken it and leave it incapable of withstanding the attacks of the very foes against whom they had gone forth to do battle. There was conquest also of Cyprus, and the turning aside of another expedition to Tunis so that Charles of Anjou might get his tribute from the Sultan, and jealousy and strife in council, and even a leaguing with the Saracens against each other,—and all this done by those who had vowed to strive with single purpose for the recovery of the Holy Sepulchre.

The Crusades are the quest of an ideal; they failed of their purpose, but their failure is the record of its abandonment.

Of each alike is true what Joinville frankly confesses of the seventh Crusade 'that God may say of them as he did of the Israelites, "et pro nichilo habuerunt terram desiderabilem,"' for they had forgotten him. Yet there were holy knights in this quest as in that of the San Graal, and the portrait of one who strove therein without reproach may be seen in Joinville's Life of S. Louis.

Not a writer of books, Jehan, Sire de Joinville, Seneschal of Champaigne! Once indeed in his youth he had summed up in a few pages the articles of his faith. As a man of thirty after six years of crusading he had settled down on his estate, and lived there quietly and somewhat uneventfully except for an occasional visit to Court. Fifty years later, when King Louis IX. had long been dead and canonised, he undertook, at the request of Jeanne, Queen of Navarre, 'that he would make' a book of the devout 'sayings and good works of the king S. Louis,' and as the Queen died during the four years he took to complete it, the work is dedicated to her son, the king's namesake and great-grandson, afterwards Louis X.

Simple, sincere, at times garrulous, but always kindly and cheerful is the old octogenarian's account of the days of his youth. The Crusade has receded into history; his memory fails him a little in the matter of dates; the plan of the campaign is rather involved and perhaps was not much clearer at the time. But memory awakes in delight, and details begin to crowd upon his recollection as he describes the fighting, the sieges, the dangers and escapes, and how at the battle of Mansourah he, together with the Count of Soissons and Pierre de Noville, had kept the bridge that covered the flank of the army against the Saracens, and how they were all wounded by their arrows, and how the Count of Soissons had jested, saying they would make speech of that day together in ladies' bowers; and how once being forced to surrender he saved himself and all his followers from massacre by pretending that he was the king's cousin, and how the cellarer had given his vote that they should not surrender either to the galleys or to the land forces, but should all die and go to paradise. Very vivid also the memory of their sufferings, of the fevers and diseases which attacked the army, and how as prisoners they lived in constant expectation that they would all be massacred.

He had told it all doubtless many a

time, and must soon make an end of telling it, but he is now putting together all he had known about the king; and it is a very pleasant task, and lest in the course of the narrative he should forget to introduce some of the talks which the king had with him, or to make mention of some of his acts of piety, he describes these at the outset and then tells the story of the Crusade. The Character of S. Louis as thus portrayed is perhaps the most complete embodiment of the ideal of Christian chivalry which we may find in a record of life.

He is gentle, full of solicitude for his people wherever he may be so in consistency with his vow, modest,—yet inflexible in purpose,—asking advice of his council, but not deferring to it against his own judgment, very brave — not pursuing danger but never flinching from it, — when a prisoner, unmoved by threats of torture, taking his share of all the perils that befell his army, refusing to leave the ship in which he was returning after she had struck on a rock and was considered unseaworthy, so that by his presence he might give the others courage to remain in her. Unquestioning in faith, undoubting of God's purposes but full of natural affection, he replies to the Provost of the Knights Hospitallers who had congratulated him on the victory of Mansourah that God is indeed to be worshipped in all His ways, but big tears roll down his cheeks as he speaks, for his brother the Count of Artois has been slain in the battle.

Somewhat hasty in condemning the weakness of others, and then regretting his impatience, he is himself humble in receiving reproof, and in the rules of conduct which he wrote for the guidance of his son, he bade him so to bear himself that his friends should not fear to tell him of his faults. Humble also in his failure when the possibility of success has passed away, and even as King Richard when they would fain show him Jerusalem covered his eyes and prayed that he might not look upon the holy city since he could not deliver it from the hands of the enemy, so when the Sultan offered to give sureties that he might go there on pilgrimage, he takes advice of his council and refuses, because if he, the first king in Christendom, did this, others might be content to thus fulfil their pilgrimage without delivering the holy city.

The failure of the Crusade was apparent to all after the capture of the king, and the cession of their solitary conquest, Damietta, in order to obtain his release. The chief lords of the council advised that they all return forthwith to France; and one by one they gave their advice, and Joinville, when it came to his turn, urged the king to remain, because if he departed the other prisoners would never obtain their freedom, and the king said he would announce his decision in eight days. And Joinville says that after the council was ended, all either reproached or shunned him because he had differed from them. And as he stood sadly apart looking out of the window, some one came behind him and leant on his shoulder, and put his two hands on his head. He had just told him to go away and leave him in peace, when he recognised by a ring on the finger that it was the king; and the king asked how he, who was only a young man, had had the daring to urge him to remain, in opposition to the advice of all his chief lords, and he answered that he had urged what he believed was right, and he would have been dishonest if he had done otherwise. 'If I stay shall you stay too?' said the king, and he answered 'Yes' if he could find means to live upon, and the king told him to be of good comfort for he was very grateful for his advice; and on the eighth day the king announced that he would remain, and held Joinville to his promise.

Fortitude, humility, gentleness, are all embodied in the king's conduct in this scene, and it is in the recording of such incidents that Joinville's life of S. Louis has its unique and enduring value, as the portrait of a knight without reproach, who, alike armoured or un armoured, did nothing base. As king, he ruled with justice, clemency, and wise ordinance. As son, as husband, as father he was alike loving and loved. He walked uprightly in the allotted path of human duty; yet still withal a stranger and a pilgrim. Still for him the inner dream and the quest of its fulfilment,—still hope unconquerable. He would fain again go crusading, and thirteen years later did set out with a smaller army than before, and died at Tunis,—far from the city he might not enter, yet seeking it, nor from attainment so remote but that some Pisgah-sight of promise passed before his eyes in dying.

This was the last Crusade, and after the death of the king the army all came back again, or rather such of them as the plague had spared; and there was soon enough to do in fighting Saracens in Europe, without seeking them in Palestine.

Many of those who had gone with S. Louis on his first Crusade were unwilling to accompany him again, and among their number Joinville, for he had found that while absent in the service of God and the king, his lands had been harried, his people impoverished and oppressed, and he was of opinion that he would be best doing God's will by remaining to help and defend them, and by going no more on pilgrimage. His purpose being only to write of such things as he knew he will make no account of the expedition to Tunis, for he thanks God he was not there; and so the book closes, briefly telling of the king's death and canonisation and appearance to him in a dream, and leaving us in no uncertainty as to Joinville's views about crusading.

III

In the changed temper of the old Seneschal we may discern something of the changing spirit of the age. In the years ensuing there was much difference of opinion as to how best to do God's will, or whether to do it at all,—differences only to be settled by the sword,—but unanimity among the knights about going no more on pilgrimage. Less also of a childlike inconsequence in the actions of faith, in other words less imaginative piety manifest in them; and a gradual perception that they were not so much strangers upon the earth but that it might be made a very comfortable place to tarry in,—and much effort to this end. Journeyings more practical for conquest or commerce; and other work for the sword and issues more immediate than the delivery of the Holy Sepulchre. So the knight having given up his ideal quest, and Abana and Pharpar being deemed good enough to wash in for any process of purgation that is at present necessary, the seeker of Jordan is no longer looked upon very seriously by his fellows.

Palmer, pilgrim, or romer still remained a familiar figure. Indeed on the stage of life the path seemed a pleasant enough one for a time for an actor of leisure and of a roving fancy, and served either as one of love's disguises or as a help to its forgetting; and as such, picturesque and interesting, with cockle-hat and staff and sandal shoon, for long he wanders in and out of the romances and plays of the succeeding ages, a foil to graver parts, a mark for laughter kindly or contemptuous, tricked out in antique garb and more of a mummer than his fellows, yet at times meeting with a careless glance of sympathy for memory's sake.

Aucassin in the dungeon singing of the beauty of Nicolete tells how a palmer from Limousin lay tossing upon his bed in pain and at sight of her passing by was healed of his sickness and went back to his own place comforted. We are not told whether the palmer was setting out or returning, whether his quest was completed or abandoned. To the old minstrel the quest seems immaterial. Perhaps some Nicolete of Limousin had been the cause of all his trouble and of his departing, and he was healed by the vision of Nicolete, and it did not matter much what he was looking for in the meantime. In this indifference to the purport of the palmer's journey the minstrel of the twelfth century song-story curiously anticipates the attitude of those who came after the age of questing and pilgrimage. It is a touch of the same spirit when Helena in 'All's Well that Ends Well' puts on the garb of a S. Jacques' pilgrim, but rather as a travelling costume than with any intention of visiting the saint's shrine; for from Rousillon she goes to Florence,—a very devious route to Compostella, but one which led straight to Bertram, the husband who had spurned her,—and there she found means to win his love, and so finally

> 'Journeys end in lovers meeting,'

and it seemed indeed a fit and proper way of ending all journeys, the pilgrim's journey among the rest, if he would only be a wise man and take happiness when it offered.

So gradually the age put away from itself unpractical journeyings; turned from its visionaries of faith or deed, left them on the hillsides telling '*Aves*' in their cloisters, or tilting at windmills in the plain, forgot about them or jested with their memory, or when regarding them most seriously did so with a grave compassion, as men who had put away childish things might look upon others who had played as children all their lives, and had been childlike in faith also.

'I cannot laugh at,' says Sir Thomas Browne, 'but rather pity the fruitless journeys of Pilgrims, or contemn the miserable condition of Fryars, for though misplaced in circumstances there is something in it of devotion.'

To cross Europe afoot to pray before a shrine, to encamp in fever swamps for the possession of a sepulchre,—laugh at, pity, contemn, what we will, effort so unpractical, so misplaced,—but 'there is something in it of devotion.'

The flame light of cathedral windows led us to attempt to conjecture something of the fervour of mediaeval faith, and the conjecture leads us back to a little chapel in the cathedral at Siena, the chapel of S. Giovanni.

It is scarce eight yards across, low and round, the dome blue and starred with gold, which all looks very soft and rich in the dim, gradual light. There is a font there carved by Jacopo della Quercia, a statue of S. John by Donatello, and also some small frescoes by Pinturricchio, which were commissioned by a knight of S. John of Rhodes, Alberto Arringhieri. In one of these the knight is represented as a young man in the habit of his order kneeling in prayer.

He is kneeling in a flowery meadow. In the background there is a typical mediaeval landscape, full of life and movement, hills and castles with turrets and battlements, a wooded vale and a lake beyond it winding amid the hills, and men are hurrying to and fro, and one on horseback rides with speed. 'Helmet and hauberk thou shouldst have worn, and been girt with the sword as were thy fellows,'—such was Euphemian's lament over his son Alexis who had chosen the sanctity of poverty. This knight is in full armour, and his sword is girt to his side; but he has doffed his helmet and his gauntlets and is kneeling with bared head and hands uplifted. Not the refusal of life's turmoil this, but a pause before action, and the gathering of strength which should endure questing and pilgrimage.

Vision and Memory

IN a wild glen in Devon the water leaps in riot down the crags and swirls with deep murmur over the pools. The thickets of gnarled oak and beech and ash start from the water's brim, and bending shadow it, and then wind steeply up the hillsides. The verdure is the deep full green of late summer scarred by the crimson clusters of the ash berries. On the moor above are long belts of bracken and the purple glory of heather.

The wind stirs gently in the glen, swaying with soft undulation the ferns and grasses that cluster in rock-crevices.

The soft temperate air breathes a solitude and supreme content. Only the music of the moving water breaks the stillness with its eternal note of sadness. The fascination of its melody lures from the perfect pleasure of the present to memories. Memories called from the past by some unlooked-for turn of the wheel of remembrance; memories of other scenes in other lands; of hill-sides thick with olives gleaming silver to the sun, or shrinking, scorched by its embrace; of mossy undergrowth where the air is odorous with violets; of groves of palm and cypress; of plains of miles on miles of sun-steeped vineyards and all the rich-hued pageantry of the South. And in the scene of sylvan English loveliness the wonder of the beauty of Italy seems to take a unity and meaning the more vivid by the sense of contrast. For memory sleeps but lightly, and the touch alike of pleasure and of sorrow is quick to awaken, and the light sleeper rises and hurries away, her eyes mist-wreathed with the visions of sleep, a pilgrim to the present, 'wandering between two worlds,' and bound for a goal of far endeavour.

What is this restlessness which thus draws to the South the fantasies of memory or of dream?

Heine has given it perfect expression in his lyric of the pine and the palm—the pine standing lonely on a northern height, and sighing for the warm splendour of the palm-clad South, and the palm parched beneath a southern sky dreaming of the gentler coolness of the North.

It is the more definite expression of the sense of world strangeness: the conjecture of something other than the immediate which should more satisfy the sensibilities; and in northern art and song this feeling has found expression in praise of Italy and the rich-hued glory of the South.

Praise of a visioned Italy,—an *eidolon* of thought vague as fantasy, forth-fashioned of the desire of the spirit,—seen only in dream—its ramparts as though set in sheer space, and girt by the mist of the unattainable,—the land long sought of the wanderer, to whose repeated questioning the answer was alone:

'Dort wo du nicht bist—dort ist das Glück;' but for whom the vision existed so long as his quest was unfaltering.

Praise of an Italy real and remembered—

seen in dream, but there fettered by memory. It will then lose something of the infinite possibilities of the conjectural, but will gain in vividness and dearness of recollection, for the memory of happiness will touch the chords of the soul more tenderly than they can ever be stirred by its expectation.

If essaying to realize the dream you visit visioned Italy, you make her the real, the remembered, then indubitably something is lost in the transformation. Some aspects of the vision must be modified under the pitiless logic of facts; somewhere a cold insensibility will be shown to the peculiar charm of what has drawn you in reverence and awe; something that should be Roman will be found Sardinian; some monastery that you have imaged as a sleeping phantasm of a vanished world will be used as an artillery barrack; some fresco—dim and faded in colour but changeless in purity and simplicity—will be found cleft asunder by the gaunt protruding arch of some pretentious modern tomb, or completely ruined alike in colour and outline by ill-judged restoration. Nor is the disillusionment the less poignant although you may realize that this is inevitable in a land so rich in monuments as Italy, and that in truth there is manifest in the acts of the *municipio* of every city in Tuscany a loving reverence for the past, and an attempt to preserve its art treasures and the memory of lives of good endeavour.

The sense of contrast of the reality to your half-formed visions may be such that you are like to decide as Heine did when he wrote to Theophile Gautier, 'And have you been to Spain, and can you still write about it?' that there are certain countries of the heart which are known better without seeing what masquerades as reality, which 'sleep brings close and waking drives away.'

True is this of some cities and lands which have for an age flashed as beacon-lights on the pathway of human progress, and then on a sudden the flame has grown ineffectual and quiescent, and the spent light has quivered and flickered away, and the embers have grown cold and been scattered, and only their memories abide;

or if life still clings to the spot it is as the young phoenix—posthumous,—born amid the ashes of life already departed, seeming as it were a stranger trespassing on and violating the sanctity of a tomb.

Tunis may hold the dust of Carthage in pledge, but it would be hard to part it from the sand of the desert.

Persepolis too, it is better not to visit. I have never been there and am not in the least likely to go, and my entry into the capital will always remain an entirely poetic rhapsody—

> 'It is a glorious thing to be a king
> And ride in triumph to Persepolis,'

and Marlowe's mighty line governs the ceremony. I enter riding in triumph. I am for the nonce a king. It is inconceivable that any actual visit would have other result than to blur this vision and shatter the fabric of the glory of Tamerlane.

But I cannot feel that it is better not to visit Spain in order to leave dreams intact, and even the most elegiac of those who travel there are neither tongue-tied by the sense of contrast nor yet is their utterance a lament that the past has been swept away. Rather would it seem that the hand of Time has touched the mediaeval glory of Granada and Castile very gently and reverently, mellowing it in radiance and sustaining it in sleep. And assuredly it is without question better to visit Italy and get visions modified as may be, for Italy of to-day is more beautiful than all dreams of it, and it will be the source of new visions manifold arising on the ashes of the old.

II

Yet disillusionments there will be. Perhaps the entry into Rome will be one. I forget what my chosen form of entry used to be, but I am sure it was not by train. Now, however, having had experience of that method of entry I can imagine no other, and if I speculate at all about the matter it is as to whether it will be the *diretto* or the *direttissimo* next time or whether I shall ever take a seat in the *train de luxe.* In the day of stage coaches at the end of a long drive you came suddenly to a turn in the road where the eternal city was spread out before you, pasture to your gaze, and the driver at the psychological moment cracked his whip and remarked 'Ecco Roma!' Now the railway station and the painful newness of the Via Venti Settembre hardly offer the same facilities for poetic impressions. Nor will the sense of incongruity end here. The evidence of two civilisations in the Colosseum inspired Gibbon to write the 'Decline and Fall,' as it had previously been witness of the resolve of Villani that he would put on record the history of his native city. Perhaps you have indulged the fancy that the same spectacle may awaken in you some comparatively noteworthy thoughts or resolutions, and visiting it by moonlight for the heightening of picturesque effect you have found yourself playing involuntary hide and seek with a multitude of other tourists whose existence you would fain forget, and by day you have been an unwilling listener to peripatetic lecturers. You abstract yourself from these adventitious aids: the immensity, the magnificence is and must be awe-impelling as long as the stones remain, but the girdle of beauty, the wreathings of fern and grasses, with which each recurring spring would fain pay its tribute to the enduring grandeur of the fabric, all are torn ruthlessly away by its conservators, and the arena is freshly sanded, smooth to tread upon, and the result is rather archaeological than picturesque.

The same is in a measure true of all the relics of ancient Rome. They seem huge open-air museums, impressive alike by their immensity and antiquity, but surpassed in the haunting suggestiveness of beauty by an ivy-mantled English belfry tower.

Shelley in the preface to 'Prometheus Unbound' states that: 'The poem was chiefly written upon the mountainous ruins of the Baths of Caracalla, among the flowery glades and thickets of odoriferous blossoming trees, which are extended in ever-winding labyrinths upon its immense platforms and dizzy arches suspended in the air.'

Glades and thickets are there no longer

No glint of colour in the arches. Their dull red is arid and bare as the sand beneath them. There is nothing to abstract the attention from the crumbling masonry or to hinder the realization of the fact that these were once baths and are dust baths still.

Nature is the most fitting guardian of the monuments which a vanished race have entrusted to her keeping, and conservation such as this is in very deed a defilement.

Rome has disillusionments, and yet Rome is assuredly of all museums the most fascinating.

The eternal city—time's enigma in its periodic newness of life. The eternal cities—city built upon city—Rome of the Caesars, Rome of the Papacy, Rome in her tireless activity the capital of Italy. Coming to Rome you are not a stranger, you have followed the path immemorial and inevitable, you have come to your heritage, for it is a part of the destiny of things, of your destiny and hers, that you should come and that she should teach. You have come even as your fathers have come, as all nations have come, captives for a witness of her triumph, conquering Goths to be conquered by her unarmed strength, Emperors and Kings to do obeisance to Christ's Vicar, pilgrims from far lands—barefooted and travel-stained—to offer prayers before some shrine that they might win pardon for sin, lovers of art to gaze upon her treasuries and win the thoughts that lie prisoned in her marbles. And long as is the roll of her visitants the eternal city has been justified of them and they have learnt in the measure of their seeking, if they have sought humbly and waited: the dried rod blossomed in token that Tannhäuser might be saved, but he had stayed not within the gates and knew it not.

So for centuries the human tide changeless and ever changing as the sea has surged within her gates, bringing to her its needs, its doubts and aspirations,—to learn of her fortitude to bear, of her energy to create, of her faith to suffer and to hope. Drifting on the tide, coming to your heritage, you wander amid her streets, and piece by piece, and stone by stone you make her memories your own, and unravel and remember and recreate her history and yours; and by the sorcery of dreams, temples and palaces are from the past recaptured, and 'cloud-capt' the structures of Imperial Rome float before the eye in pristine grandeur.

Then a vision no less wonderful,—the mighty dome and gleaming cross of S. Peter's dwarfing the seven hills, the mass of lesser domes and campaniles innumerable, and all around treading on the dust of Caesars a city joyous with life, a life bizarre and cosmopolitan, revelling in the sunshine of the Roman winter, streaming through art galleries, dusting sacristies with dainty dresses in the search for pictures, marching with candles through the Catacombs, crowding into the Sistine to see the Pope at High Mass, shopping in the Corso and getting the news at Piale's in the morning, and after lunch making a Rotten Row of the Pincio,—enjoying to the uttermost everything there is to be enjoyed, the concerts, the balls at the Quirinal, the opera, and the Carnival.

Wandering between these two visions you forgive much that is alien to expectation, you will forgive the conservators of classic Rome their archaeological trend, you will forgive the newness of new Rome, the huge monument to Victor Emmanuel, the unfinished Palace of Justice and the bare embankment of the Tiber, for the city still is *sacrosanct* of memory, inviolate alike to testify and to teach, and these changes are a token that the measure of her years is as yet unspanned.

III

Whatever the vision of Venice which imagination has bodied forth, the reality cannot fail of picturesqueness, and if the city be entered at dusk, the first impression is likely to surpass all conjecture. After the long railway journey the contrast is fascinating. To step into a gondola and glide through narrow waterways under low bridges whereof the lamps are reflected as stars in the still depth, hearing the slow swirl of the water round the keel, and the murmur of the ripples receding from the oar faint as retreating footsteps. To listen to the boatman's melancholy, deep-throated cry in passing canals on either hand that thread their way amid mouldering palaces dim and mysterious in the dusk. Then to emerge suddenly in the grand canal, to become one among other gondolas, gliding on the still water over the quivering shadows of churches and palaces, and on to the Lion and minarets of S. Mark and the brilliant gleam of the Piazza. This is surely the closest substitute to a visit to fairyland which can fall to the lot of ordinary mortals.

Morning brings reflection. Some of the palaces are dingy in decay, and like stage scenery lose their impressiveness in the light of day. But nothing can efface the memory of the wonder and delight of the first impression, and knowledge more minute adds to one detail the charm it takes from another. When you have settled down to see the city, and wander through churches to look at Bellinis and Tintorettos, at times gliding through the silent waterways you pass by a coign of repose so perfect, where so little of change has marked the passage of centuries, that it seems that the touch of time has ceased utterly, and that you are wafted as by some stroke of an enchanter's wand back to when the Doges 'used to wed the sea with rings,' for the water is dappling the palace steps, and the sunlight is flushing the veins of the marble portico now as in the days of the Dandolos.

The house of Othello has nothing save tradition to distinguish it from other palaces on the Riva, and yet the fact destroys no illusion.

Shakespeare's Italy is of local habitation too unsubstantial for the traveller to realize its landmarks, nor is it fashioned of the desire of dreams which recur to haunt in rivalry with the reality. For Shakespeare cannot be classed among the lovers of Italy in the sense in which some English and German poets have been. He adopted it as the accepted setting of tragedy and romance, a shadowy background, faintly outlined in the light of

Bandello and Boccaccio, but merely a background, and with nothing introduced in it which might divert the attention from the swift action of life. Local colour in plenty where he knew it—of London and Windsor—breaths of the English woodland whether the forest be Arden or a wood near Athens. But hardly any attempt to imagine local colour. Palaces and taverns were to him like enough all the world over, inasmuch as nobles and roysterers tarried in them, for they were the heart of the matter.

Whatever the story called for there were good sound models at Hampton or Eastcheap. A thick coat of local colour is apt to clog the wheel of action, and there is food enough for all moralizing in the common interests of life.

An attempt to generalize as to the conception of Italy held by the Elizabethan dramatists must rather have reference to the characters than the cities where the scenes are laid. We may say that they looked upon Italy as a land of quick moving human passion and infinite caprice of fate, but that Italy was hardly a geographical expression, that amongst the outlying parts of it must be numbered Sicily and Illyria, and Vienna as being the scene of 'Measure for Measure,' and also surely, by the fitness of things, sea-girt Bohemia. In short as a local habitation it is 'airy nothing,' but the life of it is common to all humanity.

Hence if memories be wakeful at Amalfi—set amid the golden orange groves on the Bay of Salerno—they dwell rather upon the vicissitudes of the little republic—mistress of the sea before the mighty days of Pisa's power—than upon the sad fate of the duchess in Webster's great tragedy; and at Padua, so fascinating were Giotto's frescoes in the Arena Chapel, and those from the Apocalypse by Giusto Padovano in the Baptistery, that I confess I gave no thought to ascertain the possibility of seeing the house of Petruccio; and if Verona be the inevitable exception and call up thoughts of the Montagues and the Capulets, and if Juliet's balcony be a disappointment, probably the illusion so dispelled was derived as much from the Lyceum as from Shakespeare.

IV

The words of the tablet on Casa Guidi in memory of Elizabeth Barrett Browning are true of other poets also. They have made golden links between Italy and England.

Impelled by the desire of dream, they have wandered from city to city, and the arts and memories there enthroned and the beauty of earth and sky have been as draughts from some Pierian spring of inspiration.

Milton's lines on Vallombrosa have led many a traveller there, and will do until the forests are all cut down. And the wanderings of 'Childe Harold'—to how many have they been a pilgrimage?—a dear pilgrimage of thought? And when following on the paths of vision you are face to face, the stanzas have a trick of recurring, for there is that about them that will endure to meet the reality, and their stately chiselled beauty becomes the more apparent.

Rich in memories of Byron, of Shelley,

and of the Brownings, is the whole expanse of Italy, from Asolo to Naples, from Venice to Lerici, and it is in the valley of the Arno—river of poets—that their memories cluster most thickly. By years of wandering they gained to know Italy in the infinite variety of her beauty. The details of this knowledge more familiar are revealed rather in letters than in song. Therein they would fain reveal the spirit.

Thus to wander is indeed to know Italy—a knowledge not to be won in Rome or Florence. There the past is side by side with the present. In the old-world cities of Umbria and Tuscany you are the sole intruder. All else is steeped in the sleep of centuries. Sentinels of a vanished past, silently they testify—for the stones speak if you read of their carving—testify of the ambitions and beliefs of the builders, of a national life, strong and self-reliant.

Cities of the mountain and cities of the river.

Cities of the mountain—perched on eyrie fastnesses amid the tumbling hills, established in Etruscan strength that dug deep into the living rock before ever the Roman legions came, and whereof the grip still holds—unchanged of aspect, save that above the walls rise domes and slender campaniles, and in the old temples of strange worship, the Madonna reigns—and now the altar and the crucifix have put on age like a garment, and are in concord with the past.

Of the cities of the river, Pisa may serve as a type.

There is something of the lover's devotion to his mistress in the worship by the city of the river. The stateliest palaces were set by her side that they might gaze upon her. The span of the bridges seem as circling arms that would fain embrace. The lamps that deck her are as a gleaming carcanet of gems. She was girdled with gates to seaward. She watched the galleys go forth to battle, and welcomed the victors home. It was in her chapel to 'Our Lady of the Thorn,' that the sailors' votive offerings to the Virgin were laid.

A little distance apart in a quiet grassy space by the city wall lies the frescoed cloister of the sacred field of death, and beside it are the chief monuments of Pisan art,—the baptistery, the cathedral, and the campanile bending graciously. A place of reverie, and a solitude.

The roads that lead to it are grass-grown, and it seems that the city has turned away and clings rather to the lady of life, the river, to gaze upon her and listen to the music of her voice.

They have grown old together, the lover and the lady,—old, wrinkled and quiescent. There are no Pisan galleys now to take the sea. The still surface of the river is unruffled, and asleep in its silent depth lie the trembling images of palaces and mouldering towers. The city too is asleep, dreaming of the past, and the song of the river is the quiet music of memories. But when the storm rages in the Apennines and the streams sweep in torrent to the plain, the Arno rises hooded in her might, and in the dark swirl of the rushing river the wrinkled image is as a dream dissolved, and the city trembles and seems as though it would wake, and waking, die.

Pisa has many memories of deeds and thoughts that live: the site of the Tower of Famine, the lamp which Galileo watched swinging, the relief from which Niccola Pisano learnt something of the old Greek manner of carving, the convent of S. Anne, where was imprisoned Emilia Viviani—immortalised in 'Epipsychidion.'

One may wander through the pinewoods to Gombo, where the sea gave up the body of Shelley, or on a long spring morning, farther afield to Lucca, crossing the brow of Monte S. Giuliano which hides it from the Pisan, or following the winding valley round its base; and all along the path the meadows are paven with flowers, and their arrowy odours mingle in the fresh spring air, steeping the senses in an ecstasy of delight.

Of the beauty of these old-world cities, as of that of hillside and valley, vision is no forerunner. For vision wins not nature to her aid, and cannot tell her secrets. Her dream may dim the reality in its conjecture of the master-works of man the builder, of 'cloud-capt towers and gorgeous palaces,' but she cannot image the beauty seen in autumn and spring wanderings in the garden of Italy, the glory of the Umbrian sunset, the silver belt of Como winding among the beech-clad hills, the first pink flush of the peach-blossom in the Tuscan valleys. So whether it is that conjecture has hardly dwelt upon the lesser cities, or that the immobility of their life has made them seem a part of nature, the sight of the many towers of Albenga or San Gemignano is a delight unmingled by the sense of contrast.

Art is the utterance of beauty, and in art has the beauty of Italy rendered to the Giver its tribute of wonder and praise. It is the utterance of things by the wayside, of things lowly and familiar and therefore chosen of beauty to be her ministrants. The stone from the quarry becomes a gargoyle in the church, or frets the sky in pinnacles.

Pigments from earth and sea are prepared and blent in the semblance of the Madonna — an altar-piece to which the eye turned restfully,—Mary Mother, august to intercede, divine and pitiful. Yet withal a girl tender with the grace of human loveliness, and the type Florentine or Lombard, for the fairest maiden in the village had sat to the painter, and it is her beauty which still lives in his picture, as type of the Maiden of Bethlehem, and the attendant saints were her family and friends, and they or rather their children's children are by the roadside or in the Piazza to-day, and the painter's art as here revealed has been 'the touches of things common, till they rose to touch the spheres.'

It is a well-known story how Cimabue saw Giotto on the hillside drawing sheep, and asked his father to let him take the boy to Florence and teach him to be a painter. Without under-estimating Giotto's indebtedness to Cimabue, let us not forget the early years when he drew sheep on the hillside. Giotto himself seems never to have forgotten them, and the memory is at the root of his naturalism. He continued all his life to draw sheep and sheep dogs, and shepherds whenever the subject of a fresco admitted of his doing so. In the Arena Chapel at Padua, there being forty-eight spaces in which to paint scenes from the lives of the Virgin and of Christ, he fills six spaces before painting the birth of the Virgin, and three of these are scenes in the desert introducing sheep and shepherds.

Of other painters learning not only in the studio but on the hillside and in the valley, we must know the footsteps before we can in a measure estimate or appraise.

Fra Angelico in his cloister at Fiesole or San Marco—who is said to have always prayed before taking up his brush—painted men as angels, and his are the pale pure colours of the sky at dawn.

Perugino's pictures breathe the gracious silence of the sunset in the Umbrian hills, and there too, amid the vine and olive, are the sylph-like aspen poplars of his backgrounds.

This gracious silence Raphael knew, and added to it tenderness, and in Rome grew his later manner,—the mastery of form and luxuriance of beauty of 'the School of Athens' and 'Attila.'

So to wander over valley and hillside, high in the Apennines on Falterona's ridge, or following the pathways of her waters down to the pine-fringed shores, to Pisa and Ravenna,—so to wander is to learn something of the footsteps of Italy's greatest sons, wanderers alike in vision and in life.

V

Vision and memory—they are the two books of all our wanderings. The one is a winged flight of imaginings, the other a treading in the pathway of experience. And in the pathway are set stones of stumbling, while in the winged flight there are no unforeseen discomfitures, and yet after all our visioned wanderings we come back no wiser than we went; we have seen what we took with us to see, neither more nor less, without let or hindrance. The book of memory is rather a record of changing purposes and changed impressions, and a recognition of the measure of our dependence upon things as mundane as hotels, and as variable as weather. And indeed of the things which are written under this latter rubric there is often a wide discrepancy between the two books, for in visioned wanderings it never rains at inconvenient seasons, and the record of memory witnesses that even in Italy the climate is uncertain, and that our purposes vary with it. At one time we have put about the helm and run before the storm; at another seeing what we went out to see, we have nevertheless not seen it, for we have seen only a rain-washed travesty of that which is itself only in sunlight.

It dies hard—but of many deaths at last dies the belief that the sky is always blue. Venice and Capri were the only places in Italy whereof in the book of memory it was written that there was always halcyon weather. And alas for Venice recently revisited! I am almost minded to go no more to Capri.

And yet who would wish, having seen it, that the sky of Italy should be always blue? Bewitching in its very uncertainties, in spring at its loveliest, it is as changeful of expression as ever a face may be. Overcast, doubting, pouting, and then breaking into smiles sweet as fugitive, and to the chasing away of the smiles follows the radiance of calm. Such is April—sunshine, shower, gloom and beauty all commingled, like an English April, laughing and weeping, only in contrast more abrupt, more southern, more passionate.

It is this Italy of which Tennyson sang in 'The Daisy,' perhaps the most realistic of all descriptions of Italian travel.

All the way across the plain of Lombardy it was raining,—and he chronicles the fact unflinchingly:

> 'Rain at Reggio, rain at Parma;
> At Lodi, rain, Piacenza, rain.'

There is something about the lines which seems to impart a vague comfort in the experience of similar weather elsewhere in Italy.

Of course it rains, and of course there are disappointments and discomforts in travel, and experience is a consciousness of things trivial.

Sunshine and shower,—and the abiding memory is not of the shower:

> 'O love, what hours were thine and mine,
> In lands of palm and southern pine.'

Ruit hora,—hours of the palm and pine—yes! and hours of the myrtle as well. And passing leave us a little older, a little wiser perhaps, probably a little sadder,—and the richer in the infinite treasure of what is written in a few pages of the book of memory. *Ruit hora*—and yet the writing is so fresh that it is hard even to believe that it was written yesterday.

Memory is a regret,—and as such is something dearer, and more intimate than vistas of the unknown:

> 'O love, we too shall go no longer
> To lands of summer across the sea.'

Vision and memory—two names serve as types of the variance of their gifts. Rossetti, in spirit a mediaeval Italian, a contemporary almost in art of Fra Filippo, in poetry of Guido Cavalcanti, and as such a dweller all his life in the Italy of vision, although he never set foot within the gates of her present-day reality.

Browning, knowing Italy by years of wandering--her mountains and valleys, her churches and art treasuries—and yet no

Italian at all, but only a lover—a lover of beauty drawn in wonder to the South as a pilgrim to the East might journey—an Englishman loving Italy. See how he loved her:

> 'Italy, my Italy!
> Queen Mary's saying serves for me—
> (When fortune's malice
> Lost her Calais)
> Open my heart and you will see
> Graved inside of it, "Italy."
> Such lovers old are I and she,
> So it always was, so shall ever be.'

Undiscovered Islands

IT would perhaps be possible to estimate how in each of the seven ages of man the thought of a small island has a several and distinct fascination; but without differentiating so minutely let us consider its attractiveness in childhood, youth, and age.

It is the bourn whither are tending innumerable voyagers on rafts improvised in the nursery or on the garden pool. Later on the narrow confines of nursery and pool are more clearly seen, and attempts to reach it are not made so lightly. But it is thought about and read of. It always has a treasure; if of precious stones or ingots it is guarded by genii; but a good store of gold pieces and fights with pirates are in general preferable as affording a fairer scope for the exercise of those qualities which lead to kicking goals and bringing off hard catches in the long-field; and in the night, in the silence of the dormitory, when sleep has parted the curtains of the matter-of-fact, a boat puts out from the port of dreams, and inky fingers grasp the tiller, and flushed arms toss and grapple with the counterpane as with pirates for the treasure.

The struggle is over, the buccaneers have retreated with their wounded, the treasure has vanished, and only the blurred outline of a dream remains, when the bell has roused the dreamer to the daily routine of work and play; which he follows with thoughts distracted by a desire to know what the next chapter holds in store.

The intrusion of a petticoated being into these romances of pirates and treasure causes an immediate and just feeling of indignation. The hero will probably become mawkish and sentimental. He will cease to court adventure with *abandon*, and the upshot will be as tame as that of a love tale. Whether or no this falling away actually takes place is immaterial. The spell is broken; the reader imagines the worst. He cannot trust the hero, whom no thunderbolts of Mars could daunt, to pass unscathed through the fire of soft glances, any more than he could trust himself to stand firm under a like assault. A fellow-feeling might lead him to judge with a standard less severe, and yet—granted the inconsistency — this instinctive recognition of the incompatibility of the two sources of interest does credit to his critical judgment.

Love is a taskmaster all absorbing,—the *fons et origo* of its own episodes of adventure—and when the sails are set on a course that love directs, the pirates' hoard is passed lightly by, though the gold gleam never so ruddily.

Yet the difference is only a choice of islands. Palm-clad homes of treasure lie mirrored in the wide expanse of the Caribbean Sea. Cythera in the Ægean saw Aphrodite first step from sea to sand and from sand to shore; and now that her visits have grown rare in cities busy with new forms of piracy, less romantic and more profitable than those of old, her votaries turn to seek her in islands where the woodland still savours of her presence, where 'a light of laughing flowers along the grass is spread,' as in the days when she first broke forth flower-fashion, where the waves along the shores still murmur, in broken melody, of the infinite mystery and wonder of her ways.

The voyage is long, and amid unknown waters, and unless love be with us at the start we shall never make the passage.

I remember seeing in the Louvre Watteau's picture of the 'Embarkation for Cythera.' The colour is soft and pleasing; the grouping is rhythmical, almost operatic; but it is obvious at a glance that the voyagers will never reach the island.

When in the morning of life two set out together, whose hearts are lit with the sunshine of a single purpose, the journey is withal a hard one. The gay Court bevy are in no mood for such a hazard. They will float down the river to Saint Cloud, and make believe that amid the lawns and fountains of the park lies Arcadia;—or is it Dresden-China land? Gallantry and persiflage will flourish freely, and a return to Court is easy when *ennui* supervenes.

They pass with their pleasuring; but Cythera abides and will still abide, a 'far Eden of the purple East,'—the *eidolon* of lover's thought;—and when Shelley in the highest ecstasy of love pours out to Emilia Viviani the vision of a future when their souls shall mingle and be transfigured,

> 'It is an isle under Ionian skies,'

to which his thought flies over-sea.

> 'The blue Ægean girds this chosen home,
> With ever-changing sound, and light and foam,
> Kissing the sifted sands and caverns hoar;
> And all the winds wandering along the shore
> Undulate with the undulating tide.'

There a pleasure-house built by an Ocean King in the world's young prime awaits them, and thus he pictures what their life shall be:—

> 'We two will rise, and sit, and walk together,
> Under the roof of blue Ionian weather,
> And wander in the meadows, or ascend
> The mossy mountains, where the blue heavens bend
> With lightest winds, to touch their paramour;
> Or linger, where the pebble-paven shore,
> Under the quick faint kisses of the sea,
> Trembles and sparkles as with ecstasy,

> Possessing and possest by all that is
> Within that calm circumference of bliss,
> And by each other, till to love and live
> Be one.'

Love impels to visions, solitude and the dreaming of dreams; and nowhere can dreams find fairer haven or solitude seem more of a reunion with primal nature, than when the bourn is girt round as with Love's own cestus by the gracious inviolate sea.

If the vision thus portrayed in 'Epipsychidion' were suddenly realized, and we were carried as by Fortunatus' wishing-cap to a desert island, the result might be with us as it is in 'Foul Play,' that most delightful of all Charles Reade's romances, where the hero is perplexed between an intense enjoyment of the charm of the situation, and an uphill struggle to preserve the conventionalities.

In 'Foul Play' the lovers return eventually to England, and the curtain falls upon a prospect of uneventful domestic felicity which promises little of island adventure.

This is, in general, true when the process of settling down takes place. There shall be no more dallying in Scyros with Deidamia; neither must Achilles linger in his tent. The course is then straight sailing and delays are of greater import. There is a cargo in the hold, and the time and profits of each venture have to be calculated before it is undertaken.

A month in summer in the Hebrides, or a yachting cruise round Scilly, may perhaps be given as hostages to the never-to-be-fulfilled fantasies of the past; but it is a tribute to the memory of the dead. The barrister or merchant can never make believe as would children that he is doing other than having a holiday. The routine of activities is but suspended. Letters are waiting for him; arrears of work are growing in his absence. The trumpet-call for him is not to the unknown of adventure, to the pursuit of an ideal that mocks yet allures,—but to the sterner virtues of practical life.

When back in town the tan of the sun and the sea-breezes will be noticed and envied for a few weeks, and then this will fade, and all will be as before. We seem made to follow some plough. Habit is the surest antidote to inordinate fancy. Maybe that the potter's vessels are awry, but when all have wrinkled lips it is better to curl and be content. Wings of Daedalus! No! There are no Icarian flights. It is too late to be ambitious. Bow the knee in the temple! They are all bowing: few remember even that they once stood upright.

As years pass, and steps begin to go down-hill,—on an incline at first scarce perceptible, but growing steeper as it proceeds, —pleasure lies more in reminiscence, and youth may have a dearer store of memories connected with it than has riper age. Grandfather and grandson have often more in common with each other than with the generation that intervenes. The elder man may be more tolerant of those differences of opinion which naturally accompany the stages of life's journey. He is the more prone to make allowance in that he sees his own youth in clearer perspective. Castles in Spain are rare of attainment, but he sees now that they may form beacons of endeavour more ennobling than do mansions in Park Lane.

Maybe he has been successful in life; maybe he has frequently been passed in the race by those of greater powers of intellect or application; in either case he is weary of the struggle. He is still a seeker; with something of a rejuvenescence of fancy his thoughts may again fly over-sea. But he would fain cherish no illusions now. The days of treasure-hoards and knight-errantry are over; he seeks only for rest.

Garibaldi having won for Italy the kingdoms of Naples and Sicily, refused all proffered titles and aggrandizement, asking only to return to his island home in Caprera.

As rest is a fit crown for the greatest of the triumphs of life's action, even so is it a solace for discomfiture and defeat. This sundering of ourselves from the scene of our activities, our fathers have told us, is as the setting out upon a voyage.

Peace lies beyond the waters. So Arthur, when his wound was deep, was borne

> 'To the island-valley of Avilion,
> Where falls not hail or rain or any snow,
> Nor ever wind blows loudly,'

that there he might find healing.

So too a Viking when smitten unto death would be laid restfully in his galley and wafted over the viewless deep, and lost to sight of man would be numbered among those who had entered Valhalla. Where time is not nor any change at all; only that on entry the ravage of years shall be undone, and the ichor of youth shall again pulsate in the veins.

Essentials these of rest; and rest holds in it the vision of a fairer excellence than ever action can compass, and, as Ruskin has said, man's longing for it is at once evidence of his origin, and a promise of that reunion when the 'I become' of the created shall merge and be transfigured in the Creator's 'I Am.'

Peace lies beyond the waters. Are the waters always those of death?

Our fathers thought not so in the days when in the desert places of the sea lay islands virginal and untrod. When credulity had in it no savour of reproach, and tradition was as a harper voicing the sea-stories and wind-stories that now float round our ears intangible and unheeded. Somewhere in the unknown,—was the message of the harper's song,—east of the sun and west of the moon, or buttressed by the surges of the Atlantic, or far as 'ultimate dim Thule' lay an island where the years pass and men wax not old. Seers dowered the island in thought with virtues elsewhere broken and inconsequent. Poets sang of the land where there is no death.

The belief was common to many mythologies—Norse, Celtic and Greek—and it survived after Christianity had spread over Western Europe.

The story of S. Brendan, the Navigator, who sought for seven years for the Land of Promise, took rank as the Christian 'Odyssey,' and the recital of the perils and wonders of his voyage charmed alike court and cloister; monks lovingly transcribed the legend in a hundred monasteries, and a Trouvère sang of it at the bidding of Adelais of Louvain, the Queen of Henry Beauclerc.

The paradise for which S. Brendan sought was an island in the West. He may have passed near where the fabled Atlantis sank beneath the waves.

The abbot and his monks reached the same islands every year in time for the four Christian festivals; as was foretold by a messenger in the Paradise of Birds,—fallen angels these, who sang on earth to the praise of God until such time as they should return to the skies.

They saw Judas chained in Promethean fashion to a lonely rock,—and there allowed relief from the torments of hell on each recurring Sabbath and on holy feast-days. They suffered perils from icebergs and monsters of the air and of the deep; and at length, when the seven years of their pilgrimage were completed, it was given unto them to enter within the darkness which lay about the land of promise of the saints,—a land where there was no night at all. They wandered for forty days amid the fair expanse of verdure, coming at last to the banks of a great river; there a youth of great beauty appeared, and told them that they might not cross, bidding them return to their own country.

They obeyed and returned to their ship, and three months after leaving Paradise, sighted the Irish coast.

Was America the paradise of S. Brendan? And the great river the Mississippi? And the islands those of the West Indies?

A tradition among the Indians in Florida told of white men who had come over the sea in times far remote, and the first settlers sent out by Admiral Coligny found the same belief among the natives of Brazil. These places are far to the south of the recorded limits of the voyages of Leif and Biarne and the later Norse discoverers.

S. Brendan was born in A.D. 484, and between the possible date of the voyage and of the earliest existent record, centuries intervene. We may weave fantasies, but we cannot build,—the fabric is as gossamer. The narrative may be only a monkish adaptation of the Celtic legend of the voyage of Maeldune, from which some of the incidents are derived. The details are doubtless imaginative; but that S. Brendan did make voyages to the West is confirmed by Adamnan in his life of S. Columba, where he speaks of his visit to Hinba near Iona.

Is it permissible to accept the legends of the early Church for the spiritual truths which they convey? Or when an abbot after years of pilgrimage finds the land of promise of the saints, must we—gazetteer in hand—identify it with a local habitation and a name, or else refuse all credence? If so, reason has itself become a fetish.

Or was it some island in the West that S. Brendan found,—primitive, inviolate, and therefore a paradise? The Spaniards interpreted the legend in this way, and cherished hopes of finding again S. Brendan's isle. A king of Portugal even made cession of it in the treaty of Evora, 's'il la découvrait.'

In the popular belief it lay to the west of the Canaries, and had on rare occasions been seen from the isle of Palma;—as on the Aran Isles the peasants have seen the meads and palaces of Hy Brasil far away over the western sea. But the eyes of the city-bred are misty or filled with other visions, and see them not.

These legends,—S. Brendan's and the like,—if they have no basis of historic fact to win for them credence, originate in the instinct and abide in the imagination of those who live within sight and sound of the sea; who, faring over great waters, and learning of their changeful magic, of the elemental fury of the tempest, and the divine soft-moving calm, think in their simplicity that an island, such as the mind of men has been able to conceive and the winds to whisper of, may not be a wonder too great to lie hidden in some unfurrowed coign in the bosom of the pathless mysterious ocean.

The breath of tradition made audible held the ear, and guided human purpose: thus fitful attempts were made to reach S. Brendan's isle, the last being in the year 1723.

Juan Ponce de Leon also, giving faith to an Indian legend, put out on the deep to seek the isle of youth's renewing; and of his quest and of its ending Heine sings. After a life of adventure he had been made governor of Cuba, and there his thoughts turned bitterly to the days of youth, recalling how as page in the court of Don Gomez he had borne the train of the Alcade's daughter; how when a courtier, the ladies of Seville had flocked to the windows on hearing the tramp of his steed; how he had wrought deeds of knightly valour against the Moors; had accompanied Columbus in his second voyage to carry the power of the Cross and of Spain across the sea; had sailed and fought under Ojeda and Bilbao; had been with Cortez when he had conquered Mexico, and in that venture, though stricken with fever in the swamp, had gained much treasure of gold and pearls.

Thus waking the memories of the past, all riches, all honours that he had won seemed to him as nothing as compared with the fact that the vigour of youth had fled; and he prayed to the Blessed Virgin to shake wintry age from his limbs, to bid the sun fire his veins and the spring his breast, to touch with roses his cheeks and his hair with golden flame, and to give him back his youth again.

Now Kaka, the old Indian nurse who tended the knight's hammock, was wont in rocking it to sing a song of her people about the isle of Bimini. 'Fly on, little birds! Swim on, little fishes!' it ran, 'be our guides to the isle of Bimini; we follow with barque all-garlanded. In Bimini the delight of spring abides continually, and the lark is ever warbling in the azure. Fair flowers grow there as herbage, and tall palms stretch their fan-like leaves above them, making soft, cool shade. There springs the loveliest of all fountains, whence flows the water that makes all things young. A withered flower touched with this water blooms with fresh beauty, and a dried rod bears leaves; and the old when they drink of it become young, shedding the mantle of age as a chafer sheds his shell; and they remain there always, for happiness and spring hold them enthralled. This land of eternal youth is the goal of my longing and desire. Farewell! farewell! dear friends of my homestead. We return no more from Bimini.'

The knight heard ever this song between waking and slumber, and the strain would mingle with his dreams, so that he murmured in sleep of Bimini; and by-and-by he decided to go in search of this Bimini that he might drink of the promised water. Many, hearing of his purpose, were minded to go with him, so that a fleet of five sail was fitted out. Others who remained behind through fear of the perils of the voyage besought them that having found Bimini, they would return and give them to drink of the water, that they too might be young again.

So with banners flying and the salute of many cannon, they sailed away on their quest.

The chroniclers who tell of the expedition of Ponce de Leon, say that he failed to find Bimini, but discovered Florida; and that there the old days of fighting as under Cortez were renewed, and that after gaining fresh treasure and renown, he was wounded by the Indians, and returned to Cuba to die.

It would seem that the thirst for adventure was still uppermost, and the fountain of youth was only desired as a means to indulge it. His hand still itched for the pommel of the sword, by which he had lived and by which he died. It may have been that he regarded the fighting in Florida merely as an interlude, and even as death found him he was in thought preparing to resume his quest. Ideals once formed are hardly ever quite abandoned, however action may digress. They will issue forth on a sudden from some disused thought-chamber and startle us with their strangeness, and seeing the vision of our past endeavour we turn to follow it. Complete disillusion or attainment are alike rare, and it is merciful that our imaginings abide, and that we travel on to the grave dreaming of things we know not of.

Heine has more of the truth than the chroniclers in his description of the ending of Ponce de Leon's voyage: –

'And he sought for youth's renewal
Ever daily growing older,
And all wrinkled, worn, and wasted,
Came at last unto that land,

To that silent land, where chilly
Under shadowy cypresses
Flows a stream, whereof the water
Hath a wondrous power of healing.

Undiscovered Islands

Lethe is the water namèd,
Drink of it and thou forgettest
All thy sorrows: yea! forgotten
Wilt be thou and all thy troubles.

Blessed water! blessed land!
He who reaches it forsakes it
Never more:—the land of Lethe
Is the real Bimini.'

Deo
Soli
Invicto

> 'Who doth ambition shun,
> And loves to live i' the sun. . . .
> Come hither, come hither, come hither.'

NAY, but you shall keep pact in coming, exile of the greenwood! Though you would still palter with the infirmity—here the air is alien and it shall find no nurture. Corn and wine for you—the lotos in Lotos-land. You shall shun ambition in forgetting, and it shall wither parched in the sunshine. Sun-steeped the days of your tarrying—wave and woodland smitten through with sunlight—glowing and trembling in ecstasy. You too, of mood ecstatic. For you shall 'live i' the sun' I warrant you, and worship him with every fibre of your being. If

Arden of the greenwood this,—an island Arden, and therein the meeter for exile, and for the sway of the sun-god to work wonderment. See his domain more closely!

It is an island about five miles long and two miles wide. The coast rock-precipice for the most part; but two landing-places,—Marinas little and big—though neither big enough for anything more than a fishing-boat to come to shore. A welcome there if not an anchorage, and on landing at such port as the isle affords, you are met by a crowd of eager islanders—eager not to know what news you bring, but only that you stay and dwell among them.

Rough paths strike up the hillside, and winding steeply amid orange groves and the mossed walls of vineyards, soon arrive at the capital.

From the big Marina a carriage-road starts on the same journey, and wanders more deviously and deliberately in the pretence that there is really hardly any hill at all. In about half-an-hour it also arrives at the capital looking quite as hot and much more dusty than the paths, and enters the gate with a rather dejected air, seeming to say that had it known before starting what a tumble-down irregular unkempt sort of village the capital would prove to be, it would never have taken the trouble to come to it from the big Marina and the fishing-boats and the daily steamer, and so indirectly from the ocean-highways from numerous points all over the earth's surface.

Being there, however, it wanders about to see any sights that may be worth seeing; and having to stoop under low arches, and be wedged in between houses which ignore its existence and try to meet above it, and only finding a breathing-space in the market-place, it finally turns away and climbs with some difficulty the side of the taller of the two hills between which the capital lies ensconced. On reaching a city on the hill-side, it stops altogether, lost in an ecstasy of contemplation, and indeed the view over-sea is so varied, so infinite, so beautiful, that there would be the rather cause for wonder if it ever came away and after looking there partook again of things less lovely. For to be always going on is surely only the settled indolence of habit, and it is quite as useful, and infinitely more pleasing for those who travel on them that some roads should, as the end of their activities, contemplate Naples, and not all crowd unnecessarily towards Rome.

Leave it contemplating! And let us glance at a few characteristics of the island's story. They are as tapestry silk-woven, shot through and through with sunlight. Warp and woof they glitter, they change hue as you mark them. Fact turns fantasy. It must surely be undiscovered, for they touch the fantastic.

The beauty of its women folk is manifest and historic, and as such exceeds description. Emperors and kings have built palaces there. Pirates have enriched it with their presence. They are said to have contributed indirectly in suggesting the present site of the capital by demonstrating how inadvisable it was that it should be any nearer to the landing-places. The buccaneers would doubtless have come if it had been a real isle of fantasy, but their absence can hardly have been remarked by the islanders, so effective were they who came in their stead. More romantic perhaps, more alluringly inexplicable, the buccaneers of the Caribbean—but for consistency in piratical endeavour match who can the Barbary Corsairs!

Another chapter dealing of combats, the writers of the island's story derive pleasantly enough from the open book of games.

It tells how two travelling companies played together at French and English. They had all the stock accessories, and played just as the game always is played on an island—with intercepted convoys of provisions, and a beleaguered garrison, hungry and finally capitulating—and with an unguarded pathway up the cliff for the attacking company, up which they scrambled by night and had a big cannonade. There was even a fleet in an offing—becalmed there of course, and consequently unable to come and relieve the beleaguered garrison; but it was a happy thought to put it there and add to the possibilities of conjecture. The breeze might spring up; the fleet might move; in a few hours it might be in action and place the besiegers between two fires. And so they knew that it was not a time to spare powder.

The issue of the contest was regrettable, and quite contrary to the best traditions of the game. The breeze grew interested and tried to help both sides. It brought the fleet quite near and then turned round suddenly and drove it away, and coming back with it after a few days, found that it had over-estimated the staying power of the garrison and that the game was ended. The English were the garrison and the French were the besiegers and consequently the ending was incorrect. This proves that it is merely a record of fact and of fighting. The wind that blows around the isles of fantasy would have surely blown otherwise. But personally I don't much regret that the ending was incorrect. English garrisons have a habit of remaining, and but for the issue of this contest they might have discovered that the island was indeed on the road to Nowhere, but that Nowhere was a far port to steam to, and that it would be well to have a coaling-station on the road.

And then they or their successors would be there still, and the island would be nothing like so picturesque or peaceful as it is at present.

No! I don't in the least regret their departure. Who could regret it at sight of the island now trembling and glowing in the sunlight? Who could regret the fighting either or anything that has ever happened there? For all these doings dark or fantastic have been but the precursors of this present, and as such become fair in reminiscence in the wonder of the sunlight.

The turbid waters have settled now in calm. The records of the island's story tell no more of fighting. The militia even look peaceful when they meet. They meet so rarely that the swords must surely ere this have been turned into pruning-hooks, and so it is in the vineyards that they have prepared for the invader, and he for his part has come with like friendliness.

Amid the runnels of the hills are olives and cytisus, and almonds pale and radiant in blossom as sun-flushed snow. Round and about are tumbling ruins and towers dismantled and the rubble of old-time masonry. Here is a roofless crumbling shepherd's hut, there the fragments of a Roman watch-tower. Alike they moulder in the sunlight, and the brown lizards wriggle among the flat stones of either impartially or lie burnishing their backs in the heat.

A deep dark blue of sea and sky—scarce varying in hue—the one limitless, quiescent, changing imperceptibly from night to day, the other ever moving and murmuring, touched in iridescence by sun and star. And the sea on the rocks has worn grottoes with roofs and walls of strange colouring of agate and red sea lichen. But of these, the blue grotto surpasses in beauty all the rest, for the sea and sky have combined to give it of their colour, filling the misty cave with quivering phosphorescent light.

The mention of the blue grotto surely places the identity of the island beyond cavil or questioning.

Sirens, palaces, pirates and fighting—these are the accessories of numberless islands, some in either hemisphere, others in the seas delectable 'cast beyond the moon,' to be found or no, as the wind may list, but assuredly to be sought for; but seek how you will, there is only one blue grotto, and the island is quite easy to be discovered, because of course it is Capri.

Capri is quite as real as the Isle of Thanet. And the Sirens dwelt there and sang to Ulysses. It was either there they sang or else on the rocks that lie to the south of the headland facing Capri, and Ulysses must have heard their singing as he passed through the strait. His wanderings are about as historic as the landing of Hengist and Horsa, and as of Ulysses it is not claimed that he landed, we may fairly be content with less proof of his presence. However, admitting the Sirens to be mythical, there is no doubt about the reality of Tiberius and the palaces, or of Barbarossa's castle and the visits of the Saracen pirates, and the French and English did certainly fight there, and the English were undoubtedly defeated. They were commanded by Sir Hudson Lowe of S. Helena fame and they held the island for

Ferdinand IV., the Bourbon King of Naples, after the French had already started Italy as a group of republics with fanciful nomenclature, and were carving it up again into kingdoms. The French captured the island through a night attack almost as brilliant as the storming of the heights of Abraham, and at the critical juncture the British fleet lay becalmed off Ponza.

So the carriage road which we followed from the Marina up to Ana Capri and there left contemplating, did indeed look on the real Naples. Real and yet too fair for reality as seen far away over miles of gracious silent sea—a water-lily resting on the marge—the fairest of the flowers that girdle the bay with beauty. For the cities there all seem as flowers: Massa, the little sea-pink on the rocks, Sorrento, cool and muffled in orange groves, Torre del Greco and Torre Annunziata, roses lying on Vesuvius' mantle, happy, forgetful of Pompeii, as the rose forgetful of the rose of yester-year, and the lily's bud Posilipo, and Pozzuoli, a marsh-flower on the waste where the Mantuan found Avernus. They seem as flowers up-tilted to the sun. And Capri, the centre flower, cupped with green, up-tilted, up-straining—more than a flower—a sanctuary. What wonder if its story be the record of things fantastic!

There are temples there, of faiths passed over. Tiberius built twelve during the years of his retirement; to his gods presumably dedicate,—or in inception merely palaces of pleasure such as that in Xanadu. Tiberius's doings in them were certainly not calculated to propitiate any deities whosoever. Some fragments remain,—notably the huge ruins of the Villa Jovis—a mass of crumbling walls and arches, luxuriant in broken marbles and mosaics. And nature has encompassed it with a perennial veil of beauty, and it has lain there for nigh two thousand years crumbling and mellowing,—and yet withal it seems an exotic.

Whether it be palace or temple it is alien to the inner history of the island, as alien as Tiberius and all the Emperors. And Jove as a tutelary deity is of power more finite than the builder. For Tiberius is still a little bit alive, and being more discriminating now than in the days of vanity, is only a terror to evildoers. They know of Timberio. Just as the Arab children, years after the Crusades were ended, knew that King Richard still rode in Palestine, and trembled at night to think of it. But evildoers are so rare in Capri that Timberio's appearance must needs be infrequent. It was this Tiberius Caesar whose friend Pilate had preferred to be; and to the Villa Jovis had been brought the news of the Crucifixion, and he had willed to enrol the Galilean among the Gods.

Gods outworn! Emperors dead and phantasmal! Temples ruined and forsaken! Yet is the island still a sanctuary.

There is a cave on the eastern hill. A temple alike rifled and bare of sacrifice, but daily the god still visits it, daily walks over the water golden-footed, and fills the cave with his presence, and touches the site of his altar with flame. Daily—even as he has come for oh! how many thousand years before ever men built altars of sacrifice! He knew the cave ere his shrine was, and knows the whole island, and daily traverses it tutelary and benignant, and he gives to the vine its fruit and to the hills their verdure, and to the islanders harvest of their works and contentment in the measure of their days. At his touch cobwebs glitter in caprice of light, and in his presence the facts of the island's story, the memories of the doings of dead men, of their comings and goings and fightings, become fair in retrospect, take on the glamour of dream as deeds done only in some visionary day. To-day seems a vision in the wonder of the sunlight, and to-morrow a mist of the sun re-risen, and yesterday a mist or vision of some extinguished sun.

Mithras! Mithras! Lord and giver of light, the giver of all the gifts of light! Mithras! The unconquered God of the Sun! And this is his temple, this cavern in the eastern cliff, outpost of the Persian's faith. Built perhaps by wanderers from the East before the days of the Caesars, before ever Rome, world-weary, and weary of her own gods, had stooped to learn of her tributaries and to gather of their faiths,—and thus learning had wavered between Mithras and Christ.

The fiat had gone forth. Even the Apostate testified to the conquest of the Galilean, and Rome put away the hesitance of Constantine, and in His service resumed her strength. But Rome was ever in the forefront. There are scenes where time touches more softly, where old customs abide and old faiths linger, and change is gradual, almost imperceptible, truth to truth added, radiance upon radiance revealed.

There are eyes,—would-be eyes of faith—which despite all their straining see as yet no farther than the sun.

Mithras may wander regretful as Pan in the woodland,—gods forgotten of worship—and yet in Capri he is not an exile. They who served him of old served him with penance and oblation, and the worshippers gathered in his temple waited while the priests made sacrifice, and together they watched and waited for the coming of the light.

And the light came, and looking down

the scarp of the cliff over the pathway of the light across the whitening sea, to where the sun had just risen above the Calabrian hills, they would see the marbles of Paestum gleaming white on the shore.

We may stand in the entrance to the cavern to-day and look from the one to the other—the temple of the Sun-god of the Persians and the temples of the gods of Greece. And 'both were faiths and both are gone,' and the sea between seems not to sever but to unite them by its murmur, linking together in memory things forsaken.

The works done in their faiths survive them. The seed of beauty broke from the heart of the rose and passed immortal from one frail dwelling to another. Greek roses bloomed in Italian soil long after that the Paestan marbles were forsaken and they grew no more beneath their shadow. Persian roses,—the murmur of their leaves in falling was ever of transience—of the transience of things beautiful and the passing of the sun-lit revel of life. And to-day the roses are blooming at Naishapur on Omar's grave, and Omar's own roses grafted on an

English stem, after nigh a thousand years, seem to have just this summer's fragrance and to mock his questioning.

Mithras's temple is deserted and the worship of all these things has passed. Yet for the Sun-god's daily beneficence, surely it is meet that we should praise him! Not with mysteries as of old; the time of sacrifice was and is not; his temple is sealed of worship. The hilltop, not the grotto! The hilltop of his own island—presence chamber of the unconquered God of the Sun!

There look down from the crest of Monte Solaro—to the south the island drops majestically to the sea, and lies on its surface mirrored and motionless, the sea beneath it treasuring in translucent pools infinite wealth of colour and of form, and all around else the island slopes away in ripple and wave of verdure down to the silver presence of the olives and the white and grey of the towns, —and beyond is the still sea, and beyond the circlets of the bays, white with cities and green with promise of the vine—and over all the gracious presence of the sun.

Deo Soli Invicto

'The earth and ocean seem
To sleep in one another's arms and dream
Of waves, flowers, clouds, woods, rocks, and
all that we
Read in their smiles, and call reality.'

Is it all a moment's fantasy, this beauty, this tremor, this ecstasy, the mirage of our vision—real only in that we behold it? Or are we alone momentary—shadows questioning sunlight—and to-morrow the same sunlight, the same beauty of earth and ocean, to-morrow and all the to-morrows all unchanged, save that other shadows thrown by the sun in his pathway will be trembling at first at the strangeness as shadows do, and then turning to follow him.

Our strength is of his strength: our moods of pleasure are of his radiance. Surely it is meet that we should praise him!

Clots of sun-illumined clay! fanned by sunbeams to a brief rapture of life, to a moment's seeming of being and begetting. Breathed upon by the wind so that we live. In the fact of our existence a sum of the sacrifices which all created things have made and are ever making for us.

And withal life is a thing pitifully fragile. Even a watch has more self-reliance, for when wound up it runs its course with composure for twenty-four hours, quietly and steadily and with accuracy sufficient even for purposes of business. How many helps we have to have to-day to enable us to take our turn to-morrow in equal freshness! How many hours of sleeping and eating and resting disconnect the brief periods of life when we are actually doing! As with one day so with all; a third of life is spent motionless in the counterfeit semblance of death, the brain fluttered by strange visions, the body, wearied with a few hours of action, seeking in sleep refreshment for the next stage of the journey. A very disconnected undertaking, and one requiring stimulus more than commensurate with result.

He is not a jealous god, the God of the Sun. We huddle together in cities and serve Baal, and the smoke of our abominations is as a cloud veiling us from his sight, and by the works of our own hands we are shut from his presence. In his presence alone is strength, and the huddled life is a poor, a half-extinguished thing. And we repent to go out humbly and seek him in his courts, and he forgives us and heals us. And we go back to the smoke of our works. And again we seek him and again he forgives us, and the flame of life burns brightly as before, or the spent flame flickers with something of its old brightness.

Surely it is meet that we should praise him, for whosoever we praise it is to the music of his pipings, and we should have but short shrift if he ceased to shine.

How nearly this once did happen, Leopardi is our authority for describing. The first hour of the day went to waken the sun as usual, and the sun declined to rise. He was in perfect health, but was weary of always going to and fro to make light for animalculae, and they might shift for themselves. The dire consequences which this resolve would occasion were urged upon him quite unavailingly. He took no interest in the existence or non-existence of humanity. If they wanted his light, they must come and get it. The morning hour pointed out that the earth was not in the least likely to feel any more energetic about the matter than his Excellency, and that after many years of inactivity she would require much persuasion before consenting to move, and perhaps a poet or philosopher might be of service in persuading her. The sun thought a philosopher would be of more use than a poet, but it would be hard to say why the earth should allow herself to be persuaded by either. So the last hour of the night went to Copernicus, who was on his terrace looking for the sunrise, and explained the predicament, and brought him back to discuss the matter.

Very reluctantly he undertook to do what he could, expecting to be burnt for his interference, but this the sun said he might avoid by dedicating his suggestions to the Pope.

There the dialogue ends. But the sunlight in my room tells me that some working agreement was arrived at, and the same sunlight makes me hope that it will be a long time before the agreement again comes up for revision.

And oh! despite all the musings of poets

and philosophers upon the inconsequence of life, if we, dreaming in the sunlight, came to believe—what of course we never shall believe—that the whole matter had been on the verge of ending, that we and all our dreams had lain but as a feather in the balance, outweighed by the momentary reluctance of the sun, then life being a thing pleasurable even in the continuity of complaining, and our hold upon it being no whit the less firm in intention as the horizon becomes more limited and the tenure more frail, perhaps we should even turn again to penance and oblation, perhaps—who knows? —Mithras coming to his temple at dawn would find it swept and garnished—and tenanted.

The Ring of Canace

SIEGFRIED by tasting dragon's blood became endued with the knowledge of the speech of birds, and at once the wood became a wood of voices warning him of the treachery of Mime the Smith.

We are no longer credulous of secrets won by tasting dragon's blood, and the understanding of bird-speech has been put away with the dragons among outworn fantasies.

Girt about by brambles more impassable, wrapped in slumber more timeless, more inviolate, than ever lay sleeping beauty in enchanted thicket, are the beliefs and superstitions of the age that is past and that we call mediaeval. We cannot enter, we cannot waken, but as we may to make questioning let us consider what impelled some of those who wandered in the wood of voices, and the talismans they bore, and the manner of singing that they heard.

The wood now seems to the infrequent passer-by a wood of brambles,—a maze pathless and thickly overgrown, where cobwebs have made a mist of the sunlight,—and if he has strayed within, the burs have clung to him, and the brambles have caught his footsteps, and the mouldering leaves have seemed dank and noisome, and he has wearied of dead decaying things, and boskage shade, and has gone back to the highway.

When the leaves that now moulder were green the wood had many pathways, and those who wandered there told strange stories of how the paths converged on a gateway, and within were glades where were heard the sounds of strange music, for the singing of birds and the speech of beasts, and the murmur of plants were all in a tongue which the visitant might hear and answer, and thus communing with nature's many voices they shared in the knowledge of her mystery in the days when the woods had pathways.

Movement and rest, sound and silence, a gathering in strength to the meridian, and a decline to sunset—they are common to all the forms of life, varying only in the time of gathering strength or combating decay, and the manner of movement or of sound.

So instinct revealed to man his kinship with all created things that in the space between their birth and death revel and wax strong in the sunlight and tremble before the fury of the tempest, and are alike resolved into dust when the life-principle passes in mystery away.

So there was fashioned forth in primitive traditions a golden age in which the speech of all living creatures had been plain, for as we read in an Esthonian folk-tale, 'at first not only men but even beasts enjoyed the gift of speech; nowadays there are but few people who understand beast-language, or hearken to their communications.'

Legends—the day-dreams of the age of instinct—told of some who in time past had gained this knowledge, of others gifted with the power from birth; and in these legends the understanding of the songs of birds took pre-eminence by the fascination of their beauty.

Belief in its possibility found expression in folk-tales, in the Eddas, and in beast-fables.

The Koran attributes to Solomon a knowledge of bird-language, and Balkis, Queen of Sheba, made her lapwing her messenger to tell him of her love. The car of Alexander is represented in legend as attended by magicians who, possessing this knowledge, revealed the future. Melampus's ears were licked by serpents' tongues, and thus cleansed they understood bird-language, and by this power of divination he was a soothsayer of high repute in all Argos. From this source the oracle Tiresias prophesied, and Cassandra drew her unregarded lore.

The knowledge thus revealed on occasion to priests and kings was shared by them with children, and as type of these legends we may select that of the boy who became Pope.

A man hears a nightingale singing and is filled with desire to know the meaning of its song. His son says he knows, but is afraid to tell. He is compelled to say, and it is that he shall be served by his parents, that his father shall bring water for him, and his mother shall wash his feet. The father orders his servants to slay him, or in some versions of the story he is thrown into the sea in an oak chest. He is saved, travels into a distant country, interprets the predictions of some ravens and is elected Pope. There are Breton, Basque, Slavonic and other versions of the story. In some versions the ravens do not predict that the boy shall be Pope, but are busy with a dispute, and by interpreting it to the king he is advanced to a high position in the court. What all the versions have in common is the fulfilment of the prediction of the nightingale that the father and mother shall do acts of service for their son.

Passing from legend wherein the interest still centres entirely with things human, and bird-utterance is somewhat similar to the utterance of the chorus in Greek tragedy,

—the attitude being that of sympathetic spectators prophesying obscurely of the development of the drama they are watching, but telling nothing of themselves and their loves and hates,—let us consider the secrets of the bird-kingdom which the magic ring revealed to Canace when she walked with her ladies in the park at daybreak. And to this end let us

> 'Call up him who left half-told
> The story of Cambuscan bold,
> Of Camball and of Algarsife,
> And who had Canace to wife,
> That owned the virtuous ring and glass;
> And of the wondrous horse of brass
> On which the Tartar king did ride.'

In 'The Squieres Tale' Chaucer tells how Cambuscan, king of Tartary, when he had reigned for twenty years held a feast at Sarra, and after the third course, as the king sat surrounded by his nobles hearing his minstrels, there entered a strange knight bringing presents from the king of Araby. For the king he brought a horse of brass, which in the space of a day should bear him wherever he pleased, or should soar high in the air as an eagle, and a sword, which could cut through armour 'thick as a branched oak,' and the wound it made could only be healed by being stroked by the flat of the blade, and for the lady Canace, the king's daughter, a Magic Mirror which should foretell adversity, and whether a lover were true or false, and a Ring of which the virtue

> 'Is this, that if hire list it for to were
> Upon hire thombe, or in hire purse it bere,
> Ther is no foule that fleeth under heven
> That she ne shal wel understond his steven,
> And know his mening openly and plaine,
> And answere him in his langage again.'

And all the nobles marvelled at the strange gifts. The horse they likened to winged Pegasus or the horse of Troy, and the sword to the spear of Achilles which could both wound and heal, and the Ring seemed to them to surpass in sorcery all others save only the rings of Moses and Solomon. And they continued in revelry and dancing until it was near the dawn.

Now the lady Canace had taken her Ring and Mirror and had early retired to her chamber, but her sleep was light and restless, for the phantasies of dream were woven around the gifts of Araby, and the space in the Mirror was in vision tenanted, and she awoke at daybreak and roused her maidens, and wandered out in the park just as the fresh ruddy light of the sun was dispelling the morning mist. She heard the birds joyously welcoming the dawn, and by virtue of the Ring which she bore on her finger she understood all their songs. Presently in her walk she came to where the woods resounded with a piteous cry, and on a tree there sat a falcon which had beaten herself with her wings until the blood had started, and had torn herself with her beak and made ever continual lament, and seemed like to swoon and fall. Canace stopped filled with pity, and held her lap to catch the falcon if she fell, and asked her why she lamented.

> 'Is this for sorwe of deth or losse of love?
> For as I know thise be the causes two
> That causen most gentil herte woe.'

And the falcon swooned and fell, and she

tended it in her bosom, and presently the falcon told her that she had been loved by a tercelet and afterwards forsaken, and for this reason she was heart-broken and wished to die.

Canace carried the falcon to the palace and made a salve of herbs for it and ministered to all its needs, glad to have found some sorrow that she might comfort.

So the hawk is left in Canace's keeping: the poet promising that after telling of the other gifts he will speak again of the Ring and of how the falcon got her love again. But 'The Squieres Tale' breaks off provokingly in mid career, leaving vistas of adventures unpursued, of wonderlands unvisited. The Ring alone of the magic gifts has as yet served its purpose in giving to Canace understanding of the falcon's sorrow; but the fulfilment of the promise of the happy ending, and the secrets of bird-language to which in the course of the story the Ring might have been an open sesame—these we can follow but with dim conjecture.

It is her own sorrow that the falcon tells,

her own life history, impact of love and grief. The pity of the blending is so after the manner of lives human as to suggest the thought that it is indeed the tale of woman's love that is being told, that the falcon was a maiden loved and forsaken, and by sorcery transformed into a bird, plaintive with the memory of her wrongs, like the swallow in her morning lay

> 'Forse a memoria de' suoi primi guai,'

and that in getting back her love again she shall be free from the spell of enchantment and resume her natural shape.

However, the Ring of Canace does not guide us so far. The bridge connecting the story with the traditions of India and Arabia, wherein the belief in metempsychosis has found expression, is a bridge spun of gossamer imaginings. Reason is too sure-footed to leave the highway. To cross it we must be buoyed up on the wings of fantasy. Guided thus we may perceive the influence of the Buddhist conception of the soul of man at his death inhabiting the bodies of different animals until the days of its sojourn on earth were completed. So all creatures were man's compeers, the dwelling-places of his forerunners in the mystery of existence, the abodes wherein for a brief space a portion of the eternal has deigned to dwell. Eastern romance drank deep of this conception and told of human beings transformed into birds or beasts by sorcery, the human life only being suspended to be resumed on release from enchantment, but who while so transformed were condemned to silence or to the use of a language known but infrequently; Beder, prince of Persia, in the 'Arabian Nights,' is transformed into a white bird, and as such is dumb, but recovers his shape on being sprinkled with magic water.

Inarticulate, unless magic ring or serpent's tongue should be an open sesame to the curious listener, bird-melody seemed nevertheless to be a striving after the expression of things human. They seemed spirits, Peris at the gate, who would fain pierce the barrier by song, and early myth fashioned forth the legends which each was striving to tell. No book has done more to perpetuate and give literary expression to such myths than Ovid's 'Metamorphoses,' which in the mediaeval age was the favourite text-book of those who sought by study to re-create the past in legend.

Significant not alone for their beauty and wealth of detail are these legends of men changing into birds and trees and flowers. They express the sense of kinship with nature as opposed to the modern study of it. We watch the phenomena of nature, her outlines, colours, murmurings and scents, and see a little perhaps of her methods, but in the ages of myth and legend men saw 'more in nature that was theirs.' The laurel turning her twisted leaves to the sun was Daphne shrinking from the forceful embraces of Apollo. Procne and Philomela retold their woes in song, and Alcyone hovered above the wave where Ceyx died. The handiwork of nature had a meaning more familiar, for all her children were moulded of like passions.

There was another glade in the wood of voices apart from the glades Eastern or Classic—a glade situate in a far recess, dewy and odorous, and visitants to it, though rare, were not unknown in the days when the wood had pathways.

Barefooted they wandered, travel-stained, worn by vigils and fasting, yet of purpose unwearied. Nothing recked they of myth or art of necromancy, spurning dragon's blood as fetish of the idolater. They may have borne Canace's Ring when they passed within the portal, but they bore it not as talisman but as emblem—emblem of purity and renunciation of all worldly self-seeking, mystic emblem of union with what is holiest, even as the ring is emblem in the union of S. Francis with the lady Poverty, or in the marriage of S. Catherine of Siena with the infant Christ.

Not touched their ears as those of Melampus by serpents' tongues: they gained not foreknowledge of fate, they won no fame in divination: touched rather it seemed by God's own finger, touched to the cleansing away of all dulness and grossness of earthly purpose, and when they entered within the portal the songs that they heard were canticles of praise.

The Ring of Canace

There is a beautiful Breton legend of a plant called Golden Herb which shines from afar like gold, which causes whoever touches it with bare foot to fall asleep immediately and understand the language of birds. It is seldom found, for it can only be seen at early dawn by such as are unsullied by aught that is evil.

For them not only in Brittany is Golden Herb growing.

Surely it grew on the hillside above Asolo, and Pippa wandering bare-footed touched it unknowingly; and so she passed, singing,

> 'Overhead the tree-tops meet,
> Flowers and grass spring 'neath one's feet;
> There was nought above me, nought below,
> My childhood had not learned to know:
> For what are the voices of birds
> Ay, and of beasts,—but words, our words,
> Only so much more sweet?'

What need of talismans for such as she?

A pure heart,—this was the Canace's ring which opened the portals to this band of pilgrims as they wandered in the dawn of faith, which made the grass gleam golden beneath their feet, the dew on it glistening with a radiance caught from Heaven, which made them to be asleep to much that it is better to be asleep to, and tuned their ears to have understanding of things that lie apart from common hearing. For these were such of the saints and fathers as bore themselves as exiles and pilgrims seeking in solitude and contemplation to attain to knowledge, fulfilling by their lives the saying in the 'De Imitatione' that 'in silence and in stillness the religious soul grows and learns the mysteries of Holy Writ; then she finds rivers of tears, wherein she may wash and cleanse herself night after night; that she may be the more familiar with her Creator.'

This attaining of knowledge more familiar was a link that drew them closer with all created things—alike children of one father, —and to the hermits wherever they wandered it seemed they were in the hollow of His hand and the birds and the beasts were their brethren. In the lives of many of the saints, of S. Guthlac of Croyland, of S. Columbanus in the solitude of the Apennines, it is recorded that birds ministered to their wants, and that they had understanding of their speech. So in the mountain fastnesses around the monastery of Alvernia the birds of the air were all friends of S. Francis; they flew around him and sang to him unceasingly, and he understood them and answered them in their language.

In one of Giotto's frescoes in the upper church of S. Francis at Assisi he is represented preaching to them. They are sitting all around on the ground and on the branches of trees, and the saint is standing talking to them very quietly and earnestly with head rather bent forward and forefinger raised in emphasis.

The sermon itself as given in 'The Little Flowers of S. Francis' has a simplicity and a beauty so mediaeval, so unique, if we except the sermon of S. Anthony of Padua to the fishes, that I cannot forbear to transcribe it. I quote from Mr. W. T. Arnold's translation.

'My little sisters, the birds, much bounden are ye unto God, your Creator, and alway in every place ought ye to praise Him, for that He hath given you liberty to fly about everywhere, and hath also given you double and triple raiment; moreover He preserved your seed in the ark of Noah, that your race might not perish out of the world; still more are ye beholden to Him for the element of the air which He hath appointed for you; beyond all this, ye sow not, neither do you reap; and God feedeth you, and giveth you the streams and fountains for your drink; the mountains and the valleys for your refuge and the high trees whereon to make your nests; and because ye know not how to spin or sow, God clotheth you, you and your children; wherefore your Creator loveth you much seeing that He hath bestowed on you so many benefits; and therefore, my little sisters, beware of the sin of ingratitude, and study always to give praises unto God.'

So S. Francis's exhortation to the birds was that their songs should be always songs of praise. But what the birds told S. Francis when they sang to him in the woods at Alvernia, of that we know not save in so far as it is written in the actions of a holy life. And before leaving the legends of the early Church let us consider what the life of S. Francis was. His life was one long benison to his fellow-men. He wooed Poverty as a mistress with more single-heartedness and concentration than we can muster in any of our wooings. His nights were spent in vigil and prayer. His sanctity and zeal in self-sacrifice were potent to draw many to give up their lives in following his precepts. We must believe that by faith followed with single purpose he had drawn nearer to God; that his eyes in spiritual vision saw perhaps farther than do our own.

We, when we hear the voices of God's earthly choristers upraised in woods and meadows, are as they who hear singing in strange unknown numbers and can but conjecture the meaning of the strain, but to him the portals of that kingdom without which we stand may have been opened, for him the songs of birds may have had meaning even as we believe they have for their Creator, whose praises they are ever singing.

The Horns of Elfland

'HARK to the horns of Elfland, blowing, blowing! *Bonne vieille*, you remember their melody, and your heart-strings thrill with it still'—thus wrote Thackeray in the Roundabout Paper 'On a Peal of Bells,' and the phrase like the horns seemed to murmur in my ears, and lay undimmed upon the tablets of memory until I met it again in the Bugle Song in 'The Princess.'

> 'O hark, O hear! how thin and clear,
> And thinner, clearer, farther going!
> O sweet and far from cliff and scar
> The horns of Elfland faintly blowing!
> Blow, let us hear the purple glens replying:
> Blow, bugle; answer, echoes, dying, dying, dying.'

The Horns of Elfland

Tennyson wrote this lyric while at Killarney, and we may assume that the heathery hills and greenest of all valleys suggested the cliff and scar, although perhaps unconsciously, his presence among them being an influence in moving the poet's mind. And so the hills wherein the horns of Elfland blow are not entirely the hills of dream.

Perhaps the melody may seem something akin to the half-heard whisper of the Celtic spirit, lamenting in its own wild glens upon the vision of a fair and unattainable past, a thing impact of the lapping of lake water and the soughing of wind and rain.

Yet fair as is Glengarriff, fair—inexpressibly fair—as is the valley of Gweedore with the Gweebara winding slowly round the base of the glittering cone of Errigal,—a green glade couched amid a wild expanse of billowy moor and peat-morass,—fair as are the fastnesses of Galway and Connemara, the hills and valleys of Elfland are something fairer, if only in that they are too elemental to have local habitation, and so are fairer even as dreams are fairer than reality, or as hope's vista is fairer than the compass of endeavour. And even as Elfland is fairer, so the blowing of the magic horns is softer yet more compelling than the music of the Celtic and alike of all other lyres.

Now before reading farther of these horns of Elfland consider have you ever heard their melody. It is better perhaps for your comfort in this workaday world if you have not; for the fatal love of the Gods has more than one gift in its dower, and there are some who have seemed to their fellows as dead when that they have heard earth-music and wandered afield with eyes dream-laden. Other melodies may have seemed to you as fairy music; they have stirred you strangely from that accustomed creature of self, and their burden has rung for a time so insistent in your ears that you have in imagination given yourself up to its dictates, and followed on the path it seemed to point out, armed *cap-à-pie*, and impetuous for whatever adventure might befall. A pictured Ferdinand for the moment treading to mystic guidance the sward of the isle of enchantment.

But the music that drew you on was not Ariel's; it led you to no Miranda; it rifted suddenly to silence amid the interstices of the wood, and left you loitering alone, stumbling amid the brambles with starved lips and weary feet, striving for a while to recapture the lost melody, and then you have abandoned the quest, petulant that fancy has lured your footsteps, have gone back to the highway, have heard again the speech of your fellows and solaced your ears that were still an-hungering. It was not the blowing of the bugle that led you on,—not Ariel's music, or if the sprite were indeed present the tune of the catch was as though 'played by the picture of nobody,' and you followed in bewilderment, a Trinculo buffeted by unseen powers. A fantasy, a trick of the ear, it called you to something apart from yourself, and you could not make the passage.

List to the blowing of the magic horn! Faintly, faintly revealed it may be, and yet the faintest of its receding echoes you will not mistake, for it sounds the dream that is within you. You may not hearken to it, and if ever unheeded its melody will become fainter, it will be a rarer visitant than when it first broke upon your ears, but it calls you to the highest that is in you to accomplish, it reveals your ultimate self. Primal nature in some mysterious unfathomable communion with that part of itself which is within you, has weighed your capacities and perplexities, has outlined forth what may be the result of endeavour, and the vision thus foreshadowed to which hope aspires, and which, though you may not as yet attain, you may keep undimmed, a glittering lodestar of your quest,—this it is to which the bugle calls you.

If you heed not the call, if you abandon that self unseen and eternal for the self ephemeral, you have so far as in you lies made the great refusal, and if the light of dawn ever parts again the curtain behind which you counterfeit sleeping and waking, and shines upon you so that you really wake, momently you will seem to realize,—

> 'O God! O God! that it were possible
> To undo things done; to call back yesterday!

—and then the vision will pass from you, you will be spared the shame of seeing what you might have been.

List to the blowing of the magic horn! Other melodies serve as preludes. For as music is the most passionate, the most sense-compelling, and the most ethereal of all the arts, so its pathway to the mind is the most intuitive and the most direct. Ear-gate is a citadel ever harder to defend than Eye-gate. Ulysses left them both unguarded: he saw the Sirens, and he heard their song, and in intention he was subjugate. If his companions had had their eyes bandaged instead of their ears being filled with wax, if Ear-gate had been left unguarded so that they had heard the Sirens' song, then they would never have rowed away.

Music by this power of dominating the senses is a prelude of thought and of melodies which the ear cannot hear.

The song or the orchestra has ceased. It has stirred you, and ceasing has left you in a tranced expectancy. Your ear strives to re-create it, to pierce the intangible web of silence and follow its echoes. But, quick as conceived, your purpose is abandoned, for there is no more silence,—only the interval is over. Maybe the opera has ceased, the curtain has fallen, the singers have been called before it, and now the orchestra have gone away to their homes, and you are walking home in the cool night air. But of silence has been formed a melody which floats around you, steeping your ears and senses with a new rich significance. For you alone is the melody. The lyre of Orpheus was never so compelling, and yet the trees around your path tower straightly up to heaven. They hear it not, or they would crouch in tremulous wonder. For you alone is the melody, for it is a part of yourself.

Not only music of man's making, but that of all nature is a prelude to the blowing of the magic horn.

The songs of birds, the cadence of moving waters, the wind lifting the leaves of trees—alike reveal it. If you are where all these have ceased utterly, still there is not silence—with your ear to the ground you may hear the faint murmur of the brown earth in travail in the quickening of life innumerable.

Nature is perpetually in a condition of music; it is an ever-changing symphony, a harmony of form and sound.

> 'Thou canst not wave thy staff in air,
> Or dip thy paddle in the lake,
> But it carves the bow of beauty there,
> And the ripples in rhyme the oar forsake;'

and when the receding ripples have won to shore, and it seems again as though keel had never furrowed the surface of the lake, still there is not silence, the moving waters have resumed their eternal melody. Eternal—yet ever changing,—at times tempest-driven to the crescendos of exultation or despair, and anon dropping to the faintest whisperings of motion. The ripple of the river ever running seaward, the beating of the waves upon the shore, the lapping of lake water, all are the recurrence of a rhythm that has been from the beginning, that has murmured in the ears of those before us, and will murmur when we have passed away like shadows, and as we in our transitory day meet the symbol of this eternity, its note wakes the chord responsive in our being and calls into action that within us which is most unfettered by the things of time.

Water seen far beneath has also an inevitable suggestion of music. From the summit of the pine-clad hill the lake lies apparent, motionless in argent ecstasy. The trees on its banks, dark against the gleaming water, bend down and jealously shut in the sound of its whisperings that they may not reach my ear. The air is silent, trembling to the sun, and downward gazing I am drawn Narcissus-like to the mirror of imaginings, and the tremor of the air is as the faint beat of wings made audible, and it gathers to a cadence that seems

> 'Like an Æolian harp that wakes
> No certain air, but overtakes
> Far thought with music that it makes;'

and the far thought is in part a memory, in part an expectation, and the memory is of a dream, and the expectation is of the dream's fulfilment, and the music takes me a willing captive, for my heart-strings are ever thrilling with its melody.

Oh to dream ever, if this be dreaming, for thus to dream is to know more truly than waking ears may hear or eyes may see!

Ros Rosarum

IT was in Prospero's enchanted island that Gonzalo told about that commonwealth of his and its Utopian virtues. 'Had he plantation of the isle,'—and then he fell to thinking what he would do. 'Full of noises, sounds, and sweet airs' the island,—yet for Gonzalo it was but an old fancy that they recaptured, and the commonwealth was not a dream first heralded by Ariel's music, but a tale oft repeated. One judges this to be the case because Gonzalo was an old man, and old men are more prone to recur to the dreams of youth than to have new fancies, and because obviously the other lords in attendance on the king had heard him tell the tale before. Their comments anticipate the text. They knew just the point at which the thread would be riven by the gusts of conflicting excellences and the latter end of the commonwealth would forget its beginning. Moreover, this very attempt to combine incongruous virtues, to load the body politic with more than its due equipment of members, shows that the would-be maker of the constitution owed no debt to Ariel's music, which—however fleeting—is yet at harmony with itself,—and lo! here are the incompatibilities.

> 'No sovereignty,—'
> 'Yet he would be king on't.'

No wonder Gonzalo's commonwealth never grew unwieldy, but remained eminently portable, so that he was able to carry it about with him all his life, from Naples to the island and from the island back to Naples, and I know not to how many cities and islands else. And he the maker was cicerone to whoever would enter,—and like the Ancient Mariner constrained the guests,—yet made no long narration, for the listener soon pointed out that the ship of state was unseaworthy in dry dock, and could not even take the water. Dear to the maker its every beam, seaworthy or no, and he left the listener turned critic. He would not have much else to do with the commonwealth beyond finding listeners to hear about it, until he had taken heart to discard one of its incongruous virtues. Bitter the parting belike, but we must give up something in compromise to the actual. No ship of dreams ever came to the immortal port with all her cargo in the hold. Not purposefully abandoned maybe, only left until the ensuing voyage at some port of call that we think to revisit, and the next voyage is in waters unfamiliar, and the dream —borne a little way and then left—is carried on by another mariner.

Even in an isle of fantasy we may not hope to unite all the republican virtues, and yet have kings and queens. In this particular choice I should never share the hesitance of Gonzalo, for I would give up all the distinctively republican virtues twenty times over for real kings and queens, if only in order that there might be no incongruity in the presence of princesses and the usages of chivalry. This only serves to show that the incompatibilities in my island are not Gonzalo's. There are hesitations there too —enough and to spare.

For alas! we are all the Gonzalos of our own isles of fantasy. Our entry would produce chaos. Our purposes are irreconcilable. No sovereignty—and yet we would be kings. This it is that makes lives come to nothing—halting ever on the brink of achievement.

This—and not that the endeavour is visionary. Follow the vision—follow the fair vision—and the more fugitive the farther belike your course. For one life lost in the far sea where the lone star beacons, how many thousands have beaten the surge 'twixt sea and shore with ineffectual hands!

'The desire of the moth for the star'—useless striving—emblem of vain endeavour, and yet it flies higher than do other moths,—far above the smoke and flame of the candle.

Seekers of things visionary—star-struck moths—they discern the highest and seek it in the measure of their strength.

And oh! the stars are so far away, and the measure of strength at best so halting and frail, that there must be no falterings of purpose in the flight.

For many one star, and on each seeker one ray falling, and this the predestined pathway of the flight. They who have soared the highest are they who have kept the pathway. Single the vision seen. Single the thought attending. Strength has been theirs to renounce all else.

> 'Other heights in other lives, God willing,
> All the gifts from all the lives, your own, Love.'

As yet one oblation—for this life is all too brief for the fashioning of one gift meet of service.

Seekers of the ideal! We look with curious eyes at the pathways wherein they sought, in quest of things immaterial, of honour in deeds, of love, of faith, of things than these more visionary, 'things impossible and cast beyond the moon.' Single the vision seen—yet ever the manner of the seeking has been but in the measure of their strength, halting and frail. If happiness has attended them in the quest it has come as a gift unexpected, unsought. Peace they have known—but only the peace following long endeavour, peace too deep for conjecture. And withal to aspire and ever to aspire nor conscious know attainment. And yet of this what know we?

Whatever is loveliest in the memories of deed, whatever is loveliest in the treasures of art and song, whatever in the beholding brings us nearer than aught else to the

> 'Dim vision of the far immortal Face,
> Divinely fugitive, that haunts the world,
> And lifts man's spiral thought to lovelier dreams,'

these—all these—are but the broken endeavours, the stammerings of the tongues, the fumbling of the hands of such as have striven of single purpose to behold. Only the gifts that they would fain fashion when near to the presence. And we are led in dream of their offerings. And in their lives they have wrought so wondrously. What of thought unexpressed? How may we conjecture of their dreams? How of the vision that their eyes have looked upon?

Of some of these quests we make no longer manner of following. They are meet only for the days of mediaeval enchantments, and such enchantments are all outworn,—all except the last enchantment of their memory. The wiser now in refusal—wise only in despite. 'Alles ist gleich, es lohnt sich Nichts—es hielft kein Suchen, es giebt auch keine glückseligen Inseln mehr.'

Gonzalo never found location for his isle, but Prospero found an 'isle fortunate' in his isle of banishment. These followers of the vision are like the rather to Prospero. Single purpose is as potent as magic art.

The quest of the beautiful is eternal. 'For ever wilt thou love, and she be fair.' The ideal was before you sought.

It drew forth the soul of Faustus to its lips, and men shall dream of Helen in ages yet unborn. No pursuit is ever abandoned. No ideals are ever as though they had never been. No quest but shall have ending upon some visionary shore.

> 'But each man murmurs, "O my Queen,
> I follow, till I make thee mine."'

. . . . .

Of their works: Deep in the deep heart's core, of all the roses is the mystic incommunicable essence which vibrates through each petal, charging it with form and colour and fragrance, so that the rose is impact of all these qualities and they become symbols of its presence.

Paradise in Dante's 'Vision' is shaped as a pure white rose, and the centre far within is a sun of light that makes radiant the whole, and the petals circling outward leaf by leaf are the courts wherein dwell the assembly of the saints. The white rose this of leaves eternal.

There are roses upturned towards it—roses of man's making that live long after they who have fashioned them, and in fading fade not wholly.

Some of these are the roses of mediaeval beauty. The scattered leaves are still fragrant.

Some are white and untroubled of years, some red as though they who had spent their lives in growing had watered them with their own heart's blood. Yet of such watering cometh not their fragrance. These are the roses on which the dew has fallen.

www.ingramcontent.com/pod-product-compliance
Lightning Source LLC
Chambersburg PA
CBHW021142090426
42740CB00008B/903
* 9 7 8 1 5 2 8 7 0 8 8 6 9 *